BLACK'S

Writing
Dictionary

T.J. Hulme   **T.F. Carmody**   **J.A. Hulme**

A & C Black · London

The compilation of this dictionary has been helped considerably by the many class teachers who have co-operated with us. We are most grateful for their help, and for the help given by various Primary and Secondary Head Teachers, College of Education Lecturers and, most of all by the children themselves.

TJH   TFC   JAH

Reprinted 2006, 2008
Second edition published 2003 by A & C Black Publishers Ltd
38 Soho Square
London W1D 3HB
www.acblack.com

© 1962 and 1972 TJ Hulme, TF Carmody and
JA Hulme

First edition published in 1962
Reprinted 1973, 1974, 1976, 1977, 1978, 1980, 1982,
1986, 1988, 1990, 1993, 1996, 1999

A CIP catalogue record for this book is available
from the British Library

ISBN 978-0-7136-6512-3

Printed and bound in Great Britain by Caligraving Ltd, Thetford, Norfolk.

A & C Black uses paper produced with elemental chlorine-free pulp, harvested from managed sustainable forests.

Contents

The following list shows the page number for each new letter of the alphabet:

About this dictionary

Black's Writing Dictionary is designed specifically to help writers who need quick access to correct spellings. It is meant to help anyone who needs to speedily find or check a spelling so that they can focus on writing fluently. The words listed are the most common 8,000 words, especially those that may cause difficulty. So, a word like cat is not mentioned whereas catch is included.

A writing dictionary is not like other dictionaries. It is not cluttered up with 'parts of speech', or information about where a word came from. Its aim is to make finding a spelling as simple as possible. Once confidence is gained, a more conventional dictionary might be used.

How the Writing Dictionary is organised

This dictionary is organised in the same way as most dictionaries – in alphabetical order. The top of each page gives the first two letters of the words on that page. So, if you were looking for the word fun you would skim through the f section until you found the page headed fr fu This page has some words that start with fr and some that start with fu

What does the dictionary provide?

This dictionary provides most of the words that you will need when you are writing. It gives correct spellings, the meaning of the words and other words that are related.

The entries are arranged in three columns:-
1. In the left-hand column you will find the basic word in red.
2. In the middle is a simple definition.
3. The third column provides words related to the basic word that might cause spelling difficulties. These are written in bold, black type, e.g.

chew	to bite with teeth	**chewed** **chewing**

Plurals that might cause spelling problems are given in red in the third column, e.g.

city	a large town	cities

Note:
Where the entry can be a noun or a verb, the spelling of the plural is given, in red, alongside the noun meaning. The spelling of the third person singular, is given alongside the verb meaning, e.g.

address	1. the place where someone lives	addresses
	2. to write an address	**addressed**
	3. to speak to	**addresses**
		addressing

Where there might be confusion about the use of a word, it is listed as normal and also given in a sentence, e.g.

brought	(John *brought* his satchel to school yesterday)

Ideas for using the Writing Dictionary

When people say, 'I find writing hard', they usually mean 'I find spelling difficult'. To help make writing easier, the dictionary could be used in the following two ways.

1. Look up words during writing. This works best if you can use the dictionary speedily and have a pretty good idea of how to spell the words.

2. While writing, attempt any difficult words and underline them. After writing, use the dictionary to help check and correct.

How to use this book

Let's pretend that you are looking for the word damp.
1. Find the section that stars with d.
2. Look down the list of words in red on the left-hand side of the
   page until you come to -

damp	slightly wet

That was easy because damp comes near the start of the d words.

However, there is a faster way to find words than looking through
every word in each section.

Let's suppose that you want to find the word pond.
1. First find the section that starts with the letter p.
2. Pond begins with the letters po, so look at the top of the page
   and keep turning until you come to po.
3. Now start looking down the left-hand side until you find -

pond	a small lake

Use the alphabet for a quicker search

All the words are listed in alphabetical order. The dictionary starts
with words that begin with a, then b, then c and so on. Look at the first
letter of the word that you want to find. Will this come near the start
of the book, in the middle or towards the end?

Suppose you are looking for the word tonight. The letter t comes
towards the end of the alphabet, just after r and s. This means that
you can flick through the book for the letter t at the top of each
page, near the end of the book. Get used to flicking the pages quickly
and looking at the top of the page for the section that you need.

Each section is ordered alphabetically as well. This means that bat comes before beg because a comes before e. This can also help you find words quickly. If you are looking for by-pass then look towards the end of the b section because y is near the end of the alphabet. If you are looking for the word baby then look near the start of the b section, because a is near the start.

Can't find a word?

Sometimes the word that you want may not be on the left-hand side of the page. Instead, it may be on the right-hand side in bold, black letters. These words are based on the red words and may be hard to spell. They are all part of the same family.

Let's suppose that you want to find the word dusty.
1. The letter d comes near the start of the dictionary. So, first find the d section.
2. Now look at the top of the page for du. It will come near the end of the d section.
3. Look down the words listed for dusty. You will soon find dust written on the left-hand side.
4. Look on the right-hand side for dusty.

dust	1. a fine powder in the air 2. to remove dust	**dusted** **dusting** **dusty**

There are a few words in red on the right-hand side. These are words in the plural that have an unusual spelling. Most words just add on the letter s so that <u>cat</u> becomes <u>cats</u>. However some words add on es (a church – some churches) or change their spelling completely (a mouse – some mice). These are written in red because they can be tricky.

mouse	a small rat-like animal	mice

Ideas for spelling

Many people who find spelling hard have been helped not only by using this dictionary, but also by developing more strategies for spelling, e.g. you can:-

• Say the word slowly and listen to the sounds that you can hear. Break the word up into each sound, rather like a robot speaking! Write down the letter or letters that represent those sounds, e.g. smash = s-m-a-sh

• Think of a rhyming word, e.g. If you can spell crash then this might help spell smash, as they share the same ending.

• Take each bit at a time, by breaking the word into syllables. (Remember, every syllable has a vowel or a y in it). smash has one syllable   smash/ing has two

• Get used to jotting the spelling down on a notepad. Look at it carefully. Does it look right? If not, try again until it looks right.

• Is there a word related by meaning (e.g. if you can spell ear then you can spell hear)?

• Does the word start or end with a common beginning or ending (e.g. in, un, dis, ex….ing, ly, ed)?

• Is there a rule that you know (e.g. when you add ing onto a word that ends in e, then drop the e as in move - moving)?

• Does using grammar help (e.g. a verb in the past tense is probably spelled jumped and not jumpt)?

• Invent a catchy way to remember spellings, e.g. Because = Big Elephants Can Always Understand Small Elephants.

• Ask a friend or use a spellchecker.

• Look up the word in Black's Writing Dictionary.

• Never dodge a useful word - have your best go and keep writing!

Pie Corbett

a

abacus	a frame with beads on wires, to help with counting	abaci abacuses
abandon	1. to leave somebody or something, meaning never to return 2. to stop doing something before you have finished	abandoned abandoning
abbey	a place where monks or nuns live, or where they used to live	abbess abbot
able	1. clever 2. can do something	ability
aboard	on a ship	
about	1. almost or nearly 2. to do with 3. around	
above	over	
abroad	in another country across the sea	
absence	being away	absentee
absent	away	
accept	to take what is given to you	acceptance accepted accepting
accident	something unpleasant that happens by mistake	accidental accidentally
account	1. a story 2. a bill	
accurate	exactly right	accurately
ache	1. a lasting pain 2. to have a pain that lasts	ached aching
acid	1. a very sour liquid 2. sour	
acorn	fruit of the oak tree	
acre	a piece of land the size of a small football pitch: 4840 square yards	

acrobat	a person who does clever tricks with his body, often in a circus	
across	1. from side to side 2. on the other side	
act	1. something that you do 2. to do something 3. to take part in a play	**acted** **acting** **action** **active** **activity**
actor	a man who takes part in plays or films	
actress	a woman who takes part in plays or films	**actresses**
add	1. to find the sum of two or more numbers 2. to join one thing to another	**added** **adding** **addition**
adder	a small poisonous snake: a viper	
address	1. the place where someone lives 2. to write an address 3. to speak to	**addresses** **addressed** **addresses** **addressing**
adhesive	paste for sticking things together	
admiral	a very important officer in the navy	
admire	to think a lot of	**admirable** **admiration** **admired** **admiring**
admit	1. to let someone or something in 2. to own up	**admission** **admitted** **admitting**
adult	a grown-up person	
advance	to go forward	**advanced** **advancing**
advantage	something that helps or is useful	
adventure	an exciting time	**adventurous**

advertise	to make something well-known, usually through posters and newspapers	**advertised** **advertise-** **ment** **advertising**
advise	to tell a person something in order to help him	**advice** **advised** **advising**
aerial	wire rods, often on a roof, for a radio or television set	
aerodrome	level ground where aeroplanes take off and land	
aeroplane	a machine which flies in the air	
affectionate	loving	**affection-** **ately**
afford	to be able to spend time or money	**afforded** **affording**
afraid	frightened	
after	behind: later	
afternoon	between noon and evening	
afterwards	later on	
again	once more	
against	1. on the opposite side to 2. touching; near to	
agree	to think the same as	**agreeable** **agreed** **agreeing**
aground	stuck on the sand or rock in a ship	
ahead	in front	
aid	1. help given to someone 2. to help someone	**aided** **aiding**
aim	to get ready to hit	**aimed** **aiming**
air	1. what we breathe 2. to make sure that clothes are quite dry	**aired** **airing**
aircraft	flying machine	**aircraft**
airfield	place where aircraft take off and land	

air-hostess	someone who looks after passengers on an aircraft	air-hostesses
airpilot	one of the crew of an aeroplane	
airport	a place where passenger aircraft take off and land	
ajar	open a little	
alarm	1. fear 2. a noise or shout to warn people of danger 3. to frighten	alarmed alarming
album	a book for storing stamps or pictures	
alight	1. on fire 2. to step down from something	alighted alighting
alike	the same, or nearly the same, as	
alley	a narrow path between buildings	alleyway
alligator	a short-nosed crocodile	
allotment	a piece of land used as an extra garden, usually for growing vegetables	
allow	to let: to give permission	allowed allowing
alloy	a mixture of metals	
almost	nearly	
alone	by oneself	
along	from one end to the other	
aloud	so that someone can hear	
alphabet	all the letters from A to Z	alphabetical
already	by now	
also	as well	
altar	the holy table in a church	
alter	to change	alteration altered altering
although	even if: though	

altogether	completely
aluminium	a very light metal
always	1. at all times
	2. every time
amaze	to surprise very much

amazed
amazement
amazing

ambulance	a van for carrying sick people
among	with other things or people
amount	a quantity
amuse	to make people laugh

amused
amusement

amuse oneself to pass the time pleas- **amusing**
antly

anchor 1. a large hook which digs **anchored**
into the sea bed to hold a **anchoring**
ship
2. to drop anchor

anoicnt	very old
angel	a spirit sent from God
anger	bad temper: rage

angrily
angry

angle	a corner
animal	a live creature
ankle	the joint between foot and leg
announce	to tell something to a group of
	people

announced
announce-
ment
announcer
announcing

annoy to make someone cross **annoyance**
annoyed
annoying

annual 1. a book which comes out **annually**
once a year
2. once a year

anorak	a waterproof jacket with hood
another	1. a different one
	2. one more

answer	1. a reply: the result of a sum	**answered**
	2. to reply	**answering**
antelope	an animal like a deer	
anxious	worried	**anxiously**
any	one, or some, of a number of things	**anybody** **anyhow** **anyone** **anything** **anyway**
apart	not together	
ape	a monkey	
apologise	to say you are sorry	**apologised** **apologising**
apology	what you say to show you are sorry	**apologies**
appear	1. to come into sight	**appearance**
	2. to seem	**appeared** **appearing**
appetite	a wish to have food	
apple	a fruit	
approach	to get near to	**approached** **approaches** **approaching**
approximate	almost correct	**approxi-** **mately** **approxima-** **tion**
apricot	a fruit	
April	the fourth month of the year	
apron	a cloth tied round the waist to keep one's clothes clean	
aquarium	a fish-tank	
arc	part of a curve or circle	
arch	the curved top of a bridge, door or window	**arches** **archway**
archer	a person who shoots with a bow and arrow	**archery**
area	the size of a flat space	
argue	to talk for and against something	**argued** **arguing** **argument**

arithmetic	working with numbers	
arm	1. the part of the body between the hand and the shoulder	**armed**
	2. to give weapons to	**arming**
armour	a suit to protect the body in battle	**armoured**
army	a lot of soldiers	armies
around	on every side	
arrange	to put in order: to plan	**arranged** **arrange-ment** **arranging**
arrest	to take as prisoner	**arrested** **arresting**
arrive	to reach a place	**arrival** **arrived** **arriving**
arrow	used with a bow for shooting	
artful	crafty	
artificial	not real: made up	
artist	a person who paints, or draws or carves	**artistic**
ash	1. what is left when something has been burnt	ashes
	2. a kind of tree	
ashamed	sorry for something you have done	
ashore	on land	
ask	to put a question	**asked** **asking**
asleep	not awake: sleeping	
aspirin	a medicine that helps to stop pain	
ass	a donkey	asses
assembly	a gathering of people	assemblies
assist	to help	**assistance** **assisted** **assisting**

assistant	1. someone who serves in a shop 2. someone who helps
astonish	to surprise **astonished** **astonishes** **astonishing** **astonish-** **ment**
astronaut	someone who travels in space
astronomy	the study of stars and planets **astronomer**
astride	with legs apart
ate	(Peter *ate* his dinner quickly)
atlas	a book of maps **atlases**
atmosphere	the air surrounding a planet
atom	a very, very tiny piece **atomic**
attack	to start a fight **attacked** **attacking**
attempt	1. a try **attempted** 2. to try to do something **attempting**
attend	to be there **attendance** **attended** **attending**
attendant	a person who is paid to look after a place that people use, such as a park or a swimming bath
attention	1. taking notice 2. standing straight up with feet together and arms by your sides
attic	a room in a roof
attract	1. to be very pleasing to people **attracted** **attracting** 2. to make things come closer **attraction** **attractive**
audience	people who are listening or watching a performance
August	the eighth month of the year
aunt	your mother's or father's sister **auntie** or your uncle's wife **aunty**

author	a person who writes books or plays
autograph	someone's name in his or her own handwriting
autumn	between summer and winter
avalanche	a lot of snow and ice sliding down a mountain
avenue	a road, usually lined with trees
average	the middle point between the the highest and the lowest
avoid	1. to keep away from **avoided** 2. to move so that something **avoiding** misses you
awake	not sleeping
away	not here
awful	terrible **awfully**
awkward	1. clumsy 2. difficult to handle
axe	a chopper
axis	the line or point round which **axes** something turns
axle	a rod on which a wheel turns

b

baboon	a large monkey
baby	a very young child **babies**
back	1. the opposite side to the **backed** front **background** 2. a defender in a game **backing** 3. to move backwards **backwards** 4. to give support to
bacon	part of the meat we get from pigs

bacteria	very small living things which cause disease	
badge	a decoration we wear on clothes to show that we belong to a special group, such as a club or school	
badger	a hairy animal about as big as a small dog, which digs holes in the ground in which to live	
bails	the two bits of wood placed on top of cricket stumps	
bake	to cook food in an oven	**baked** **baking**
baker	a person who makes bread and cakes	
bakery	a place where bread and cakes are made	bakeries
balance	1. to keep something steady in one position 2. scales for weighing or comparing masses	**balanced** **balancing**
balcony	1. a platform that sticks out high up on a wall 2. the top floor in a cinema or theatre	balconies
bald	with no hair	
ball	1. a round object used in playing games 2. a dancing party	**ballroom**
ballet	a special kind of dancing	**ballerina**
balloon	a very thin rubber bag which can be blown up	
banana	a fruit with a yellow skin	
band	1. a thin strip of something 2. a number of people making music together 3. a group of people	**bandstand**
bandage	1. a strip of cloth for covering a cut 2. to tie up a cut or sore	**bandaged** **bandaging**

bandit	a robber
bang	1. a loud, sudden noise
	2. to make a loud, sudden **banged**
	noise **banging**
	3. to hit
bangle	a metal ring worn on the wrist
banisters	the handrail at the side of the stairs
banjo	a musical instrument
bank	1. a building where money is **banker**
	kept safe
	2. the ground at the side of a river
	3. sloping ground
banner	a flag
barber	a person who cuts men's hair
bare	not covered **bareback**
	barefoot
	bareheaded
	barely
bargain	something bought cheaply
barge	a large, flat cargo boat used mainly on rivers and canals
bark	1. the outer covering of a tree
	2. a noise made by a dog **barked**
	3. to make a noise like a dog **barking**
barley	a kind of corn used to make beer
barn	a farm building for storing crops
barrel	1. a round, wooden container for liquids
	2. the long, narrow tube of a gun
barrow	a small hand-cart
base	1. the bottom of something
	2. place where a ship or aircraft is kept
basement	part of a building below ground-level

basket	a bag, made from cane, for carrying things
basketball	a game similar to netball
bassoon	a musical wind instrument
bat	1. a mouse-like animal that flies at night 2. a piece of wood used to hit a ball **batted** 3. to have an innings at cricket **batting**
bath	1. a tub for water in which you **bathed** can wash your body **bathing** 2. to wash a child or animal **bathroom**
bathe	to go into the sea or river to **bathed** swim **bathing**
batsman	a person who is batting in a **batsmen** game
battery	a container for storing elec- **batteries** tricity
battle	a fight between two opposite **battlefield** sides **battleship**
bay	part of the sea which makes a curve into the land
bazaar	1. an eastern market 2. a sale to get money for helping people
beach	the sand or stones at the edge **beaches** of the sea
bead	a small shape which can be threaded on a string
beak	the hard part of a bird's mouth
beam	1. a thick, heavy bar of wood 2. a ray of light **beamed** 3. to shine **beaming**
bean	a kidney-shaped seed in a pod, used as a vegetable
bear	1. a strong, hairy wild animal 2. to carry **bearing** 3. to suffer **bore**
beard	the hair on the chin and cheeks **bearded**
beast	any large four-footed animal **beastly**

beat	1. the district looked after by one police constable	
	2. to hit	**beaten**
	3. to stir quickly	**beating**
	4. to do better than someone else	
beauty	1. a lovely thing	
	2. loveliness	**beautiful**
		beautifully
beaver	an animal that lives in or near water	
because	for this reason	
become	to grow to be: to come to be	**became**
		becoming
bed	1. a thing to sleep on	**bedclothes**
	2. a garden plot	**bedroom**
		bedside
		bedspread
		bedstead
		bedtime
bee	the insect from which we get honey	
beech	a tree with a smooth grey bark	
beef	meat from bulls or cows	
been	(I have *been* busy today)	
beer	a drink made from malt, barley and hops	
beetle	an insect with hard wing covers	
before	in front of: earlier	
beg	to ask for money, clothes or food	**begged**
		begging
began	(It *began* to rain so I went home)	
beggar	a person who begs because of being poor	
begin	to start	**began**
		beginner
		beginning
		begun

behave	1. to do as you are told 2. to be good in front of others	**behaved** **behaving** **behaviour**
behead	to cut off the head	**beheaded** **beheading**
behind	at the back of: late	
being	(You are *being* good if you are behaving yourself)	
believe	to think that something is true	**belief** **believed** **believing**
bell	a metal cup, which rings when it is hit	
belong	to be part of	**belonged** **belonging**
belong to	to be owned by someone or to be part of something	
below	under: lower than	
belt	a strap which goes round the waist	
bench	1. a long seat 2. a strong table	benches
bend	1. a curve 2. to curve	**bending** **bent**
beneath	under	
beret	a soft cap with no peak	
berry	a small fruit which has seeds	berries
beside	at the side of	
besides	as well as	
best	the finest	
betray	1. to give away a secret to an enemy 2. to do or say something that you have promised not to	**betrayal** **betrayed** **betraying**
better	improved: not so ill	
between	in the middle	
beware	be careful	
beyond	further than	

bible	a collection of books about the life of Jesus Christ and the times before He was born	
bicycle	a riding machine with two wheels	
big	large	**bigger** **biggest**
bill	1. a bird's beak 2. a note showing how much money is owing	
binary	a scale of numbers using two as a base instead of ten	
bind	to fasten together	**binding** **bound**
birch	a tree with a smooth silvery bark	birches
bird	a feathered animal that flies	
birth	1. the start of one's life 2. the beginning	**birthday**
biscuit	a small thin, crisp cake	
bisect	to cut into two equal parts	**bisected** **bisecting** **bisection**
bishop	an important member of the clergy	
bit	1. a small piece 2. the metal part of a bridle, which fits into a horse's mouth	
bite	to cut with your teeth	**bit** **biting** **bitten**
bitter	sour or sharp	
black	the opposite of white: very dark	
blackberry	a small black fruit, often found in hedgerows	**blackberries** **blackberry- ing**
blackbird	a black-feathered bird	
blackboard	a board on which you write with chalk	

blackcurrant	a small black fruit, grown on a garden bush	
blacksmith	a person who makes things with iron, such as shoes for horses	
blade	1. the cutting part of a knife 2. a piece of grass	
blame	to say that it is someone else's fault	**blamed** **blaming**
blancmange	a kind of jelly made with cornflour and milk	
blank	without any writing on: empty	
blanket	a woollen covering on a bed	
blast	a rush of air: an explosion	
blast-off	the take-off of a space rocket	
blaze	1. a fire with bright flames 2. to burn strongly	**blazed** **blazing**
blazer	a flannel sports jacket, often part of a school uniform	
bleed	to lose blood from a cut	**bled** **bleeding**
blew	(The referee *blew* the whistle)	
blind	1. a screen for a window 2. unable to see	**blinded** **blinding**
blindfold	with the eyes covered	**blindfolded**
blink	to open and close one's eyes quickly	**blinked** **blinking**
blister	a swelling, like a bubble, on the skin	
blizzard	a driving snowstorm	
block	1. a large, solid piece of some-thing 2. to close up	**blocked** **blocking**
blond	fair haired	
blood	the red liquid in our bodies	
blossom	1. a flower 2. to flower	**blossomed** **blossoming**

blot	1. a spot, or smudge, of ink 2. to dry up ink	**blotted** **blotter** **blotting**
blouse	a loose top part of a woman's clothing	
blow	1. a hard knock 2. to send out air from your mouth	**blew** **blowing** **blown**
blue	the colour of a cloudless sky	
bluebell	a wild flower	
bluebottle	a large fly	
blunt	not sharp	
blush	to go red in the face, usually because you are shy	**blushes** **blushed** **blushes** **blushing**
board	1. a plank of wood 2. to get on to something that moves	**boarded** **boarding**
boarder	1. a child who lives at school except during the holidays 2. someone who lodges in another person's house	
boast	to make out that you are better than you are	**boasted** **boasting**
boat	a small ship	**boating**
body	1. a living person 2. the main part of anything	bodies **bodyguard**
bog	wet, spongy ground	**boggy**
boil	1. a painful swelling under the skin 2. to heat any liquid until it bubbles	**boiled** **boiler** **boiling**
bold	fearless	**boldly**
bolt	1. a sliding fastener, often on a door 2. to run off suddenly 3. to gobble one's food	**bolted** **bolting**

bomb	1. something filled with explosive 2. to drop a bomb	**bombed** **bombing**
bomber	an aeroplane that carries bombs	
bone	part of the skeleton of the body	**bony**
bonfire	a fire lit outside, usually in a garden	
bonnet	1. a woman's hat that ties on with ribbons 2. the part of the car that covers the engine	
book	1. sheets of paper fastened together in a cover 2. to order in advance	**booked** **booking**
bookcase	a set of shelves for holding books	
boot	1. a cover for the ankle and foot 2. the back part of a car, in which luggage is carried	
border	the edge	
bore	1. to make a hole in 2. to talk in an uninteresting way	**bored** **boring**
born	(Jane was *born* in London ten years ago)	
borrow	to get something on loan	**borrowed** **borrowing**
both	the two together	
bother	1. trouble 2. to worry or trouble	**bothered** **bothering**
bottle	a glass container for liquids	
bottom	the lowest part	
bough	a branch of a tree	
bought	(I *bought* some sweets at the shop)	
bounce	to spring up and down	**bounced** **bouncing**

bound	1. a leap 2. tied up	
bound for	on the way to	
boundary	a mark to show the outside edge	**boundaries**
bow	1. the front of a ship 2. a weapon for shooting arrows 3. used with a violin to make music 4. a knot with two loops 5. to bend forward	**bowed** **bowing**
bowl	1. a deep dish 2. to send a ball along	**bowled** **bowler** **bowling**
box	1. a container 2. to fight with fists	**boxes** **boxed** **boxer** **boxes** **boxing**
boy	a male child	
bracelet	a ring worn on the wrist	
braces	straps to hold up trousers	
braid	a woven band	
brain	the part inside the head with which you think	**brainy**
brake	1. the part of a machine that slows it down 2. to slow anything down	**braked** **braking**
branch	part of a tree	**branches**
brass	a yellow-coloured metal	
brave	full of courage	**bravely** **braver** **bravery** **bravest**
bread	food made mostly of flour and baked in an oven	
break	1. a crack or hole 2. a rest 3. to shatter: to crack	**breakable** **breaking** **broke** **broken**

breakdown	when something will not work	
breakfast	the first meal of the day	
breakwater	a wall that is built to break the force of the waves	
breast	the front part of the body, between the neck and stomach	
breath	air that goes in and out of the lungs	**breathless**
breathe	to take air in and out of the lungs	**breathed** **breathing**
breeze	a gentle wind	**breezy**
brick	a block of baked clay	
bricklayer	a person who builds with bricks	
bride	a woman on her wedding-day	
bridegroom	a man on his wedding-day	
bridesmaid	a bride's attendant	
bridge	1. a path or road built over a road or river or railway line 2. the place on a ship where the captain stands	
bridle	part of the harness that goes over a horse's head	
bright	shining	**brighter** **brightest** **brightly**
brilliant	very bright	**brilliantly**
brim	1. the top edge of something, such as a cup or glass 2. the part that sticks out around the main part of a hat	
bring	to fetch or carry	**bringing** **brought**
bristle	stiff hair used in brushes	**bristly**
brittle	easily broken	
broad	wide	**broader** **broadest**
broadcast	1. to send out over the radio 2. to scatter freely	**broadcast- ing**

broke	(I *broke* my pencil by biting it)	
broken	(She has *broken* her train by dropping it on the floor)	
brooch	an ornament to pin on a dress	**brooches**
brook	a small stream	
broom	a long-handled brush	**broomstick**
brother	(I have one *brother*, David, and one sister, Joanna)	
brought	(John *brought* his satchel to school yesterday)	
brown	the colour of chocolate	
bruise	1. a dark mark made by knocking the skin 2. to make a bruise on something	**bruised** **bruising**
brush	1. hairs or bristles fixed to a handle, for brushing or sweeping 2. to rub with a brush	**brushes** **brushed** **brushes** **brushing**
bubble	1. air with a skin of liquid 2. to cause bubbles	**bubbled** **bubbling**
bucket	a pail, usually for carrying water	**bucketful**
buckle	1. a fastening on a belt or shoe 2. to crumple something	**buckled** **buckling**
budgerigar	a brightly-coloured cage-bird	
buffalo	a kind of wild ox	**buffaloes**
buffer	strong spring which softens the blow when railway carriages or trucks hit each other	
bugle	a musical instrument like a small trumpet	**bugler**
build	to make something: to put something together	**building** **built**
builder	a person who builds	
building	something that is built	
bulb	1. a round-shaped root 2. an electric light	
bulge	1. a swelling 2. to swell out	**bulged** **bulging**

bu

bull	a male cow	
bulldozer	a powerful machine for levelling ground	
bullet	a small piece of metal fired from a gun	
bully	1. someone who hurts or frightens people 2. to act like a bully	**bullies** **bullied** **bullies** **bullying**
bump	1. a knock or blow 2. to knock into	**bumped** **bumping** **bumpy**
bumper	a metal bar across the front or back of a car to protect it	
bunch	a group of things together, such as flowers	**bunches**
bundle	several things fastened together	
bungalow	a house with no upstairs	
bunk	1. a narrow bed fixed to the wall in a ship's cabin 2. beds, one above the other	
buoy	a marker floating in the sea to guide ships	
burglar	someone who breaks into a building at night to steal	**burglary**
burn	1. the mark caused by something very hot 2. to be on fire	**burned** **burning** **burnt**
burrow	1. a hole in the ground made by an animal 2. to tunnel in the ground, like a rabbit	**burrowed** **burrowing**
burst	to break apart suddenly	**bursting**
bury	to place, or hide, beneath the ground	**burial** **buried** **buries** **burying**
bus	a motor-coach	**buses**

bush	a small, thick-growing tree	**bushes** **bushy**
business	trade or work	**businesses**
busy	active, doing something	**busier** **busiest** **busily**
busybody	someone who will not mind his own business	**busybodies**
butcher	a person who sells meat	
butter	a food made from milk	**buttered** **buttering**
buttercup	a small yellow wild flower	
butterfly	an insect with large, brightly-coloured wings	**butterflies**
button	1. a fastening for clothes 2. to fasten with a button	**buttoned** **buttonhole** **buttoning**
buy	to get something by paying money	**bought** **buying**
buzz	1. a noise made by a bee 2. to make a noise like a bee	**buzzed** **buzzer** **buzzes** **buzzing**
by-pass	a road made for traffic to avoid a busy place	**by-passes**

C

cabbage	a vegetable with green leaves
cabin	1. a wooden hut 2. a small room in a ship
cabinet	a kind of cupboard
cable	1. a very strong rope, often made of wire 2. a wire for carrying electricity
cactus	a prickly plant cacti

café	a place where light meals are served	
cage	a place in which birds or animals are kept	
cake	a sweet loaf, often with currants	
calculate	to count or find out using mathematics	**calculated** **calculating** **calculation**
calendar	a list of the days, weeks and months of the year	
calf	1. a young bull or cow 2. the back of the leg	**calves**
call	1. to shout 2. to visit someone	**called** **caller** **calling**
calm	1. peaceful: smooth 2. to make peaceful	**calmed** **calmer** **calmest** **calming** **calmly**
came	(My uncle *came* to see me yesterday)	
camel	a large animal which has either one or two humps	
camera	a box into which you put film in order to take photographs	
camp	1. a number of tents or huts for people to live in 2. to live in a camp	**camped** **camper** **camping**
canal	an artificially made waterway for boats and ships	
canary	a small yellow-feathered bird that sings	**canaries**
candle	a stick of wax which burns to give light	**candlestick**
cane	1. the thick hollow stem of reeds or grasses 2. to hit anyone with a cane	**caned** **caning**

cannibal	a person who eats the flesh of other people
cannon	1. a large mounted gun used in olden times 2. a light quick-firing gun
cannot	(If I close my eyes I *cannot* see)
canoe	a narrow boat that is paddled along
canteen	a room in a school, office or factory where meals are cooked and served
canvas	strong, coarse cloth
canyon	a very deep valley with steep rocky sides
capacity	the amount of space inside something
capital	1. the chief city in a country 2. a large letter of the alphabet
capsize	to overturn a boat	**capsized** **capsizing**
capsule	the part of a space ship in which the astronauts travel
captain	1. a leader of a team 2. an officer in the army or navy
capture	to take as prisoner	**captive** **captured** **capturing**
caravan	a small house on wheels
card	stiff paper
cardboard	stiff board made of paper
cardigan	a woollen jacket
care	1. caution: being careful 2. worry 3. to bother about	**cared** **careful** **carefully**
care for	to look after	**careless** **carelessly** **carelessness** **caring**

caretaker	someone who looks after a school or office	
cargo	a ship's load	cargoes
carnival	a happy and noisy party in fancy dress	
carol	a special hymn for Christmas	
carpenter	a person who works with wood	carpentry
carpet	a soft covering for the floor	
carriage	a coach for the road or the railway	
carrot	an orange-coloured root vegetable	
carry	to take from one place to another	carried carries carrying
carry on	to continue	
cart	a wagon	
carton	a container in which things are packed	
cartoon	a funny drawing, on paper or in the form of a short film	
carve	1. to cut meat 2. to shape wood or stone by cutting	carved carving
case	a box	
cash	money	
cashier	a person who is in charge of money	
castaway	a person who has been ship-wrecked in a lonely place	
castle	a fortress	
catapult	a forked stick with elastic used for shooting stones	
catch	1. a lock 2. to grasp something which has been thrown	catches catching caught

catch up	to reach	
caterpillar	the grub from which a moth or butterfly comes	
cathedral	a very large church	
catkin	the flower of the hazel, willow and some other trees	
cattle	farm animals	
caught	(He threw the ball and I *caught* it)	
cauliflower	a kind of flowering cabbage	
cause	to make something happen	**caused** **causing**
caution	care	**cautious** **cautiously**
cave	a large hollow in the side of a hill or cliff, or underground	
cedar	an evergreen tree	
ceiling	the roof of a room	
celery	a vegetable which we eat	
cell	1. a very tiny part of all living things 2. a room in a prison or monastery 3. a part of a battery	
cellar	a room under the ground	
cellophane	a transparent material for wrapping things	
cement	a powder used for making concrete	
cemetery	a graveyard	cemeteries
centimetre	a measure of length in the metric system. One hundredth of a metre.	
centipede	a crawling insect with many feet	
centre	the middle	**central**
century	1. one hundred years 2. one hundred runs at cricket	centuries

cereal	1. a grain used as food 2. a breakfast food
certain	sure
certificate	a piece of writing which proves that something is true
chain	1. links, usually of metal, joined together **chained** **chaining** 2. to fasten with a chain
chair	a seat with a back
chalk	a soft stone which can be used for writing **chalked** **chalking** **chalky**
chameleon	a kind of lizard which can change colour
champion	the winner of the final in a sport or game **champion- ship**
chance	luck: something not planned
change	1. money which you get back when you have paid too much 2. to alter **changeable** 3. to put one thing in place of another **changed** **changing**
channel	a narrow stretch of water between two pieces of land
chapel	1. part of a large church used for special services 2. a small church, often in a college, hospital or school 3. churches of the Methodists and Baptists
chapter	part of a book
character	1. someone in a story or play 2. what a person is really like
charge	1. to ask a certain price for something you are selling **charged** **charging** 2. to attack by rushing forward
charm	1. a spell **charmed** 2. to be pleasing to someone **charming**

chart
1. a piece of paper or card on which facts are displayed
2. a sea map

chase   to run after   **chased**
                               chasing

chat   to talk   **chatted**
                               chatting
                               chatty

chatter   to talk about unimportant things   **chatterbox**
                               chattered
                               chattering

chauffeur   someone who is paid to drive a car

cheap   low in price   **cheaper**
                               cheapest
                               cheaply

cheat   to trick someone   **cheated**
                               cheating

check
1. a squared pattern   **checked**
2. to see if something is right   **checking**
3. to stop or slow down

cheek
1. the side of the face   **cheeked**
2. rudeness   **cheeking**
                               cheeky

cheer
1. to shout in joy   **cheered**
2. to make someone happy   **cheerful**
                               cheerfully

cheer up   to become happy   **cheering**

cheese   a food made from sour milk

chemist   a person who prepares and sells medicines   **chemistry**

cherry   a small fruit which has a stone in the middle   **cherries**

chess   an indoor game played on a square board by two players

chest
1. a large box
2. the upper front part of the body

chestnut   a large tree; its nut is often called a conker

chew	to bite with the teeth	**chewed** **chewing**
chicken	a young fowl	
chief	1. a leader: someone in charge 2. first in importance	**chiefly** **chieftain**
child	a young boy or girl	**children** **childish**
chill	1. a cold 2. cool	**chilly**
chime	1. the ringing of bells 2. to make a sound like a bell	**chimed** **chiming**
chimney	a flue for taking away smoke	
chimpanzee	a kind of monkey	
chin	the part of your face below the mouth	
china	cups, saucers and plates made from a fine clay	
chip	1. a thin slice of potato 2. to break off a small piece	**chipped** **chipping**
chisel	a sharp tool for cutting wood or stone	
chocolate	a sweet made from cocoa, milk and sugar	
choice	choosing from a number of things	
choir	a group of singers	
choke	to stop breathing by blocking the throat	**choked** **choking**
choose	to pick	**choosing** **chose** **chosen**
chop	1. a thick slice of meat containing a rib 2. to cut with an axe	**chopped** **chopping**
chopper	an axe	
chorus	1. a group of singers 2. the part of a song where everyone joins in	**choruses**
Christ	a name given to Jesus	

christen	to baptise and give a baby its Christian name	**christened** **christening**
Christian	a person who believes in Christ	
Christmas	the feast of the birthday of Jesus Christ	**Christmases**
chunk	a lump of something	
church	a building where Christians go to pray	**churches** **churchyard**
chute	a steep slide	
cider	a drink made from apple juice	
cigar	a roll of tobacco leaves for smoking	
cigarette	a small roll of tobacco, wrapped round with paper, for smoking	
cinder	a burnt piece of coal	
cinema	a place where films are shown	
circle	1. a perfectly round shape 2. to go round in a circle	**circled** **circling**
circumference	the distance round a circle	
circus	a travelling show with animals, acrobats and clowns	**circuses**
city	a large town	**cities**
claim	to demand something you have a right to	**claimed** **claiming**
clap	to slap your hands together	**clapped** **clapping**
clarinet	a musical wind instrument	
clash	a loud noise of things banging together	**clashes**
class	a group of people or things that are alike in some way	**classes** **classroom**
claw	the nails of an animal or bird	
clay	sticky earth that is used for making bricks or pottery	
clean	1. free from dirt 2. to take away the dirt from something	**cleaned** **cleaner** **cleanest** **cleaning** **cleanliness**

clear	1. easy to see or understand 2. to get rid of something	cleared clearing clearly
clergy	ministers who preach in church	
clerk	a person who works in an office	
clever	skilful or intelligent	cleverly
cliff	high, steep rock, usually at the edge of the sea	
climate	the weather	
climb	to go up, by using hands and feet	climbed climber climbing
cling	to hold on to	clinging clung
clinic	a building where you go to be examined or treated by a doctor	
clip	to cut with scissors or shears	clipped clippers clipping
cloak	a coat with no sleeves	
cloakroom	a place for leaving outdoor clothes	
clock	a machine for telling the time	clockwise clockwork
clog	1. a boot or shoe made of wood 2. to block	clogged clogging
close	1. near 2. very warm and stuffy 3. to shut	closed closely closer closest closing
cloth	material that is woven	clothes clothing

cloud	1. a cluster of very tiny drops of water floating in the sky 2. a large amount of dust, smoke or steam	**cloudburst** **clouded** **clouding** **cloudless** **cloudy**
clover	a small wild plant, used to feed cattle	
clown	a funny person, usually in a circus	
club	1. a stick with a thick, heavy end 2. a group of people who join together for some purpose	
clue	something that helps you to solve a problem	
clumsy	awkward in moving	**clumsier** **clumsiest** **clumsily**
clung	(The shipwrecked sailor *clung* to a piece of floating wood)	
coach	a carriage for carrying people by road or by rail	coaches **coachman**
coal	black fuel dug from the ground	
coarse	rough	
coast	where the sea meets the land	**coastguard**
coat	an outer covering	**coathanger**
cobbler	a shoe-mender	
cobweb	a spider's web	
cock	a male bird	
cockpit	where a pilot sits in an aircraft	
cocoa	powder made from cacao beans	
coconut	the fruit of the coco palm	
cod	a large fish caught for food	cod
code	a set of secret signs or letters	
coffee	a drink made from the roasted seed of a coffee tree	
coffin	the box in which a body is buried	

coil	rope or wire wound round and round	
coin	a piece of money	
coke	coal after the gas has been taken from it	
colander	a bowl with holes, for straining things	
cold	1. an illness of the nose and throat 2. not warm	**colder** **coldest**
collapse	to fall in a heap suddenly	**collapsed** **collapsible** **collapsing**
collar	a neck-band	
collect	to gather together	**collected** **collecting** **collection** **collector**
college	a school, usually for higher education	
collide	to bump together by mistake	**collided** **colliding** **collision**
colliery	a coal mine	collieries
colonel	an important officer in the army	
colour	1. (Red, blue and green are my favourite *colours*) 2. to paint or crayon	**coloured** **colouring** **colourless**
column	1. a line of troops 2. a pillar	
comb	1. (Peter used a *comb* to make his hair tidy) 2. (Jane went to *comb* her hair)	**combed** **combing**
come	to move towards	**came** **coming**
comedian	an actor who makes you laugh	
comfortable	at ease: contented	

comic	1. a paper for children	
	2. laughable	**comical**
comma	a sign used in writing, shaped like this ,	
command	1. an order	**commanded**
	2. to give orders	**commander**
		command-
		ing
commentator	someone who describes events on the radio or tele-vision	**comment-** **ary**
commercial	1. to do with trade	
	2. an advertisement on the radio or television	
committee	a group of people chosen to decide things	
common	1. an open space which any-one can use	
	2. happening often	
	3. vulgar	
compare	to see how things are different	**compared**
		comparing
		comparison
compass	a magnetised piece of iron or steel which always points to the north	**compasses**
compasses	a tool used for drawing circles	
competition	a game or sport held in order to find the winner	**competitor**
complain	to grumble about	**complained**
		complaining
		complaint
complete	1. whole	**completed**
	2. to finish	**completely**
		completing
composition	a written story	
computer	a machine for working out difficult problems with num-bers	
concert	a musical entertainment	

concrete	cement, sand, stones and water mixed together	
condition	the state something is in	
conduct	1. to guide 2. to direct an orchestra	**conducted** **conducting** **conductor**
cone	a solid shape with a round base tapering to a point	
confess	to own up	**confessed** **confesses** **confessing** **confession**
confetti	very small pieces of coloured paper, thrown at weddings	**confetti**
conjurer	a person who does clever tricks	**conjuring**
conker	the nut of the horse chestnut tree, used for playing the game of conkers	
connect	to join together	**connected** **connecting** **connection** **connector**
conquer	to defeat an enemy: to win	**conquered** **conquering** **conqueror**
conscious	knowing what is going on around you	
contain	to hold inside	**contained** **container** **containing**
content	happy: satisfied	**contented**
contest	a competition	
continent	a very large piece of land	**continental**
continue	to keep on	**continually** **continued** **continuing** **continuous**
contradict	to say that someone is wrong in something they have said	**contradicted** **contradicting** **contradiction**

control	1. to be in command of something 2. to hold in check	**controlled** **controlling**
convenient	easy: suitable	
convent	a house where nuns live	
conversation	talk	
convict	a person who has been sent to prison	
cook	1. someone who gets meals ready 2. to prepare food by heating	**cooked** **cookery** **cooking**
cool	1. slightly cold 2. to make anything less hot	**cooled** **cooler** **coolest** **cooling**
copper	a reddish metal	
copy	to imitate	**copied** **copies** **copying**
coral	a rock-like material made up of the skeletons of tiny sea creatures	
cord	strong string	
core	the part nearest the centre	
cork	1. the bark of a cork tree 2. a stopper made from cork	
corkscrew	a tool for taking a cork out of a bottle	
corn	grain used for food	**cornflakes**
corner	where two lines, or roads, meet	
cornet	1. a kind of trumpet 2. an ice-cream holder	
corpse	a dead body	
correct	1. right: exact: true 2. to put right	**corrected** **correcting** **correction** **correctly**
corridor	a passage-way	

cost	the price of something	**costly**
costume	dress	
cosy	1. a teapot cover 2. comfortable and warm	cosies
cottage	a small country house	
cotton	thread made from the cotton plant	
couch	a sofa	couches
cough	to force out air from the lungs suddenly and noisily	**coughed** **coughing**
could	(John *could* not come to school because he was ill)	
count	to see how many there are	**counted** **counting**
counter	1. the table in a shop over which you are served 2. a small disc used for playing some games, such as tiddly-winks	
country	1. a land where a nation of people lives 2. districts away from towns	countries **country-side**
county	part of a country	counties
couple	1. two: a pair 2. to join together	**coupled** **coupling**
coupon	a slip of paper which you can change for something else	
courage	boldness: bravery	**courageous**
course	1. (Of *course* I shall go to the party if I am asked) 2. a track for racing or for some types of games	
court	1. a closed-in space 2. the piece of ground on which some games such as tennis are played 3. a place where people are tried 4. the attendants of a king or queen	**courtyard**

cousin	a child of your uncle or aunt	
cover	to hide from view: to shelter	**covered** **covering**
coward	a person who has no courage	**cowardice** **cowardly**
cowboy	a person who lives on a ranch and looks after cattle	
crab	a sea animal which has a hard shell and strong claws	
crack	1. a sharp noise 2. to split	**cracked** **cracking**
cracker	1. an indoor firework 2. a sort of biscuit	
cradle	a cot for a baby	
crafty	artful: cunning	
cramp	a painful stiffness of the muscles	
crane	1. a machine for lifting heavy masses (weights) 2. a wading bird with long legs	
crash	the noise made when something bumps very sharply into something else	**crashes** **crashed** **crashes** **crashing**
crawl	1. to creep on the ground 2. to move slowly	**crawled** **crawling**
crayon	a coloured chalk or wax pencil	
craze	something which is very popular at the moment	
crazy	silly: mad	**crazily**
creak	to make a squeaking sound	**creaked** **creaking**
cream	the fatty part of milk that settles at the top	**creamy**
crease	1. a line made by folding 2. to fold and make a mark or line	**creased** **creasing**

create	to make	**created** **creating** **creation** **creative**
creature	a person, animal or insect	
creep	to move slowly and silently	**creeping** **crept**
crew	the people who work on a ship or aircraft	
cricket	1. a jumping insect that chirps 2. a summer game, in which a bat, ball and stumps are used	**cricketer**
cried	(The baby *cried* because she was hungry)	
crime	an evil deed	
criminal	someone who does a crime	
crimson	deep red	
crisp	1. a very thin slice of fried potato 2. hard but brittle	
crocodile	a large creature, shaped like a lizard, which lives in rivers in hot countries	
crocus	a plant that flowers early in the spring	**crocuses**
crook	1. a stick bent at the end in the shape of a hook 2. a thief	
crooked	not straight	
crop	1. the produce from a field or garden 2. to cut short	**cropped**
cross	1. anything shaped like the letter X 2. bad-tempered 3. to go over from one side to the other	**crosses** **crossed** **crosses** **crossing**

crouch	to stoop	crouched crouches crouching
crow	a large black bird	
crowd	a large number of people	crowded crowding
crown	1. the head-dress of a king or queen 2. to place a crown on some-one's head	crowned crowning
cruel	taking pleasure in causing pain	cruelly cruelty
cruet	a set of pots for salt, pepper and mustard	
crumb	a small piece of something like bread	
crumble	to break into small pieces	crumbled crumbling
crunch.	to crush with your teeth or under foot	crunched crunches crunching
crush	to squeeze very hard	crushed crushes crushing
crust	the hard outer covering	crusty
crutches	long sticks that lame people use to help them walk	
cry	1. a loud shout 2. to shout out 3. to shed tears	cried cries crying
cube	a solid shape with six square sides	cubic
cuckoo	a bird whose name comes from its call	
cucumber	a long, green-skinned vege-table	
cuddle	to put your arms round some-thing and hold it close	cuddled cuddling cuddly

cuff	the end of a coat or shirt sleeve	
culprit	the one who is to blame	
cunning	artful: crafty	
cupboard	space for storing things, with shelves and doors	
cure	to make better again	**cured** **curing**
curious	1. wanting to find out 2. strange	**curiosity** **curiously**
curl	1. anything that is twisted into ringlets 2. to twist into a curl	**curled** **curler** **curling** **curly**
currant	a dried grape	
current	a flow of water, air or electricity	
curry	1. a strong tasting spice 2. a stew cooked with curry	
curtain	cloth hanging to form a screen	
curtsy	1. the way a lady bends her knees to give honour 2. to bend the knees in honour of someone	**curtsies** **curtsied** **curtsies** **curtsying**
curve	1. a smooth bend 2. to bend smoothly	**curved** **curving**
cushion	a soft loose pad used on a chair	
custard	eggs and milk mixed and cooked to form a pudding	
custom	what is usually done	
customer	a person who buys from a shop	
cut	to divide with something sharp	**cutter** **cutting**
cycle	to ride a bicycle	**cycled** **cycling** **cyclist**
cylinder	a tube-shaped object	**cylindrical**

d

daddy	a child's name for father	
daffodil	a yellow spring flower	
dagger	a short knife, sharp on both edges	
daily	every day	
dainty	neat: pretty: graceful	**daintily**
dairy	a place for keeping milk and cream, and for making butter	**dairies**
daisy	a small flower with white petals	**daisies**
damage	1. harm 2. to harm someone or something	**damaged** **damaging**
damp	slightly wet	
damson	a small plum	
dance	1. steps set to music 2. to move in time to music	**danced** **dancer** **dancing**
dandelion	a yellow wild flower	
danger	a risk: something which might be harmful	**dangerous** **dangerously**
dare	to be brave enough to do something	**dared** **daring**
dark	1. with little or no light 2. black, or nearly black	**darker** **darkest** **darkness**
darling	someone you love very much	
darn	to mend a hole by weaving cotton or wool over it	**darned** **darning**
dart	1. a short arrow 2. to move suddenly	**dartboard** **darted** **darting**
dash	1. a line like this — 2. to rush	**dashes** **dashed** **dashes** **dashing**

date	1. the fruit of a date palm tree
	2. the day of the year you can read from a calendar
daughter	a girl child
dawdle	1. to idle or waste time **dawdled**
	2. to walk slowly **dawdling**
dawn	the coming of daylight
day	1. twenty-four hours **daybreak**
	2. the hours of daylight **daylight**
	daytime
dazed	not to know what you are doing: bewildered
dazzle	to be so bright as almost to **dazzled**
	blind anyone **dazzling**
dead	not living **deadly**
deaf	unable to hear **deafness**
deal	1. a bargain
	2. an amount
	3. to give out **dealer**
	4. to do business with some- **dealing**
	one **dealt**
dear	1. high in price **dearer**
	2. much loved **dearest**
death	the end of life
debt	something owed **debtor**
decay	1. damage caused by rotting **decayed**
	2. to rot away **decaying**
December	the last month of the year
decent	respectable
decide	to make up your mind **decided**
	deciding
	decision
decimal	a tenth part
decimals	a way of counting in tens, tenths, hundredths, and so on
deck	the flat top part of a ship
declare	1. to say something very firmly **declared**
	2. to close an innings at cricket **declaring**

decorate	1. to make something look beautiful 2. to give someone a medal	**decorated** **decorating** **decoration** **decorator**
deep	going a long way down	**deeper** **deepest** **deeply**
deer	a wild, four-legged animal, sometimes with horns	
defeat	to conquer	**defeated** **defeating**
defend	to protect	**defence** **defended** **defender** **defending**
define	to explain exactly	**defined** **defining** **definition**
definite	certain	**definitely**
defy	to refuse to obey someone	**defiance** **defied** **defies** **defying**
delay	1. to hold back 2. to put off	**delayed** **delaying**
deliberate	on purpose	**deliberately**
delicate	not strong: dainty	
delicious	very tasty	
delight	to please very much	**delighted** **delightful**
deliver	to hand on to someone else	**delivered** **delivering**
demand	to ask for something and insist upon it	**demanded** **demanding**
denominator	the number below the line in a fraction	
dense	thick	
dentist	a person who looks after people's teeth	

deny	to insist that something is not true	**denied** **denies** **denying**
depart	to leave	**departed** **departing** **departure**
department	one part of a big store or office	
depend	to rely on	**depended** **depending**
depot	a place where things are stored	
depth	how deep anything is	
describe	to say what a thing is like	**described** **describing** **description**
desert	1. land where nothing grows 2. to run away from someone or something	**deserted** **deserting**
deserve	to be worthy of	**deserved** **deserving**
design	a pattern or shape	
desk	a table used for reading or writing	
despair	1. hopelessness 2. to lose hope	**despaired** **despairing** **desperate**
destroy	to ruin completely	**destroyed** **destroyer** **destroying**
detective	someone who has the special job of finding criminals	
detergent	a powder or liquid used for cleaning	
devil	an evil spirit	
dew	small drops of water which form on things during the night	
diagonal	the line joining opposite corners of a rectangle	

diagram	a drawing made to explain something	
dial	1. the face of a clock	
	2. to ring a number on a tele-	**dialled**
	phone	**dialling**
diameter	straight line across a circle, passing through the centre	
diamond	a precious stone	
diary	a notebook for keeping a record of daily happenings	diaries
dictation	writing down what is being said	
dictionary	a book of words and their meanings	dictionaries
die	to stop living	**dead**
		died
		dying
diesel	a special kind of engine which runs on oil fuel	
different	unlike: not the same	**difference**
		differently
difficult	hard to do	**difficulty**
dig	to turn over the ground	**digging**
		dug
dinghy	a small boat, often with sails	dinghies
dinner	the chief meal of the day	
direct	1. straight	
	2. to be in charge	**directed**
	3. to show or tell someone the	**directing**
	way	**direction**
dirty	not clean	**dirtier**
		dirtiest
disagree	to differ: to argue: to quarrel	**disagreeable**
		disagreed
		disagreeing
		disagree-
		ment
disappear	to vanish from sight	**disappear-**
		ance
		disappeared
		disappearing

disappoint	to be not as good as expected	**dis-appointed disappoint-ing disappoint-ment**
disaster	a sudden or great misfortune	
disc	1. a flat, round shape 2. another name for a gramo-phone record	**discotheque**
discontented	not satisfied: unhappy	
discover	to find out	**discovered discovering**
discovery	something or some place that is found for the first time	**discoveries**
disease	illness	
disgrace	1. shame 2. to bring shame on anyone	**disgraced disgraceful disgracing**
disguise	1. something that changes a person's appearance so that you do not know him 2. to change the look of a person or thing	**disguised disguising**
disgust	disliking something very much	**disgusted disgusting**
dish	a shallow plate	**dishes**
dishonest	not truthful	**dishonesty**
dislike	not to like someone or some-thing	**disliked disliking**
dismiss	to send away	**dismissed dismisses dismissing**
disobey	not to do what you are told: to break rules	**dis-obedience disobedient disobeyed disobeying**
display	1. a show 2. to show	**displayed displaying**

disqualify	to put someone out of a game or race for not keeping to the rules	**disqualified**
dissolve	to vanish when stirred into a liquid	**dissolved** **dissolving**
distant	far away	**distance**
distinct	1. clear: plain 2. separate	**distinctly**
district	a part of a big area	
disturb	to unsettle or upset	**disturbance** **disturbed** **disturbing**
ditch	a long, narrow trench for draining water	**ditches**
dive	to go down head first	**dived** **diver** **diving**
divide	to separate into a number of parts	**divided** **dividing** **division**
dizzy	giddy	
dock	1. where a ship loads or unloads 2. where a prisoner stands in court 3. a weed	
doctor	someone who treats you when you are ill	
dodge	to get out of the way of	**dodged** **dodging**
does	(Jane *does* all her work neatly)	
doll	a toy baby or child	
dollar	an American coin	
dolphin	a sea animal like a porpoise	
done	finished	
donkey	an animal like a small horse with big ears	
door	an entrance to a room or building	

dope	to make someone sleep by giving him a drug	**doped** **doping**
dormouse	a small animal which hiber-nates	dormice
dose	the amount of medicine to be taken at a time	
double	1. twice as much 2. to fold over	**doubled** **doubling**
double-decker	a 'bus with seats upstairs as well as downstairs	
doubt	1. uncertainty 2. not to be certain	**doubted** **doubtful** **doubting**
dough	bread or pastry mixture before it is baked	**doughnut**
dove	a kind of pigeon	
down	1. soft feathers 2. from a higher to a lower place	**downward**
downpour	heavy rain	
downstairs	on a lower floor	
doze	to sleep lightly	**dozed** **dozing**
dozen	twelve	
drag	to pull along behind you	**dragged** **dragging**
dragon	a monster which was thought to breathe fire from its nostrils	
drain	1. a pipe for waste water 2. to empty 3. to dry something by taking the water away	**drainage** **drained** **draining**
drama	an exciting event, or play	
drank	(Tom *drank* to quench his thirst)	
draper	a person who sells goods made of cloth	

draught	1. a flow of air in a room 2. a counter in the game of draughts	**draughty**
draw	1. to pull along 2. to make a picture of something	**drawing** **drawn**
drawer	a sliding container in a piece of furniture	
dread	1. great fear 2. to fear a great deal	**dreaded** **dreadful** **dreadfully** **dreading**
dream	to have pictures in your mind while you are asleep	**dreamed** **dreaming** **dreamt** **dreamy**
drench	to wet all over	**drenched** **drenches** **drenching**
dress	1. clothing 2. to put clothes on	dresses **dressed** **dresses** **dressing**
drew	(Lisa *drew* a picture on the paper)	
dribble	1. to flow in drops 2. to move along with a football at your feet	**dribbled** **dribbling**
dried	(Anne *dried* herself with a towel)	
drift	1. snow heaped up by the wind 2. to float along	**drifted** **drifting**
drill	1. exercises which soldiers do 2. to make a hole in something with a special tool	**drilled** **drilling**
drink	to swallow liquid	**drank** **drinking** **drunk**
drip	to fall in drops	**dripped** **dripping**

drive	1. a private road, usually between a house and a public road	
	2. (Jill will *drive* a car when she is older)	**driver** **driving**
	3. to guide or chase animals	**drove**
drizzle	1. misty rain	**drizzled**
	2. to rain very lightly	**drizzling** **drizzly**
droop	to hang down in a tired way	**drooped** **drooping**
drop	1. a small spot of liquid	**dropped**
	2. to fall or let fall	**dropping**
drove	(He *drove* his car into the garage)	
drown	to die under water because you cannot breathe	**drowned** **drowning**
drug	1. a special sort of medicine	**drugged**
	2. to give someone a drug	**drugging**
drum	a musical instrument made from stretched skin on a round frame	**drummer**
drunk	1. (The man could not stand because he was *drunk*)	
	2. (I have *drunk* a glass of milk)	
dry	1. without water	**dried**
	2. to take all the water away	**drier** **dries** **drying**
duck	1. one of a group of birds that can swim	
	2. to move the head down sharply	**ducked** **ducking**
duffel or **duffle-coat**	a jacket of coarse woollen material with a hood	**duffle-bag**
dug	(I *dug* the garden with a spade)	
dull	1. not bright or polished	**duller**
	2. slow to learn	**dullest**
dumb	unable to speak	

dump	1. a pile of rubbish	**dumped**
	2. to throw things in an un-tidy heap	**dumping**
dungeon	an underground prison	
during	while something is going on	
dusk	nightfall	
dust	1. a fine powder in the air	**dusted**
	2. to remove dust	**dusting**
		dusty
dustbin	a large container for rubbish	
dustman	someone who empties the dustbins	**dustmen**
duty	something that you should do	**duties**
dwarf	1. a very small person	**dwarfed**
	2. small	
dye	to change the colour of some-thing by dipping it in a special liquid	**dyed** **dyeing**
dying	(The flowers were *dying* because they needed water)	
dynamite	a high explosive	
dynamo	a machine for making electricity	

e

each	every one	
eager	keen	**eagerly**
eagle	a bird of prey	
ear	part of the head with which you hear	**earache** **earring**
early	in good time: the opposite of late	**earlier** **earliest**
earn	to get something by working for it	**earned** **earning**

earth	the ground: the world in which we live	
earthquake	a shaking of the earth's surface	
earwig	a small insect	
easel	a three-legged wooden stand for a blackboard or picture	
east	where the sun rises	**eastern**
Easter	the feast of the resurrection of Jesus Christ	
easy	1. not difficult 2. comfortable	**easier** **easiest** **easily**
eat	to chew and swallow food	**ate** **eatable** **eaten** **eating**
echo	1. a sound coming back and heard a second time 2. to make an echo	**echoes** **echoed** **echoes** **echoing**
eclipse	a darkening of the sun when the moon passes between the earth and the sun	
edge	the border	
editor	a person who corrects a newspaper or book before it is printed	
educate	to help people find out and learn: to teach	**educated** **educating** **education**
eel	a snake-like fish	
effort	using strength to do something	
eiderdown	a bed-cover, once stuffed with the feathers of an eider duck	
eight	8	**eighth**
eighteen	18	**eighteenth**
eighty	80	**eightieth**
either	one or the other	

elastic	a material which springs back to shape after it has been stretched	
elbow	the joint in the middle of the arm	
election	choosing by voting	
electric	worked by electricity	**electrical**
electricity	power that gives us light and heat	**electrician**
elephant	a huge animal, with a trunk and tusks	
eleven	11	**eleventh**
elf	a boy fairy	**elves**
elm	a large tree	
else	1. as well: besides 2. if not	**elsewhere**
embankment	a raised bank to carry a road or railway over low ground	
embroider	to decorate with coloured silks	**embroidered** **embroider-** **ing** **embroidery**
emerald	a precious green stone	
emigrate	to leave one country to go to live in another	**emigrated** **emigrating** **emigration**
empire	a number of countries ruled over by one government	**emperor** **empress**
employ	1. to use 2. to give work to: to keep busy	**employed** **employer** **employing** **employ-** **ment**
empty	1. containing nothing 2. to take everything out	**emptied** **empties** **emptying**
encourage	to help by praise or advice	**encouraged** **encourage-** **ment** **encouraging**

encyclopaedia a book giving facts about many things

end 1. the finish of something **ended**
2. to finish **ending**
endless

enemy someone who tries to harm you **enemies**

engine a machine for doing work **engineer**

enjoy to be pleased by something **enjoyable**
enjoyed
enjoying
enjoyment

enormous huge: very big

enough as much as is needed

enquire to ask about **enquired**
enquiring
enquiry

enter to go into **entered**
entering
entry

entertain to amuse **entertained**
entertainer
entertaining
entertain-
ment

entire with no part missing: complete **entirely**

entrance the place where you go in

envelope a paper cover for a letter

equal exactly the same **equally**

equator an imaginary line marking the middle part of the earth, exactly halfway between the North and South Poles

equilateral a figure or shape which has all its sides equal

erect 1. upright **erected**
2. to build **erecting**

errand a short journey to take a message or collect something

escalator	a moving staircase	
escape	to get away from danger or something unpleasant	**escaped escaping**
especially	most of all	
essay	a composition: a written story	
estimate	to guess approximately what you think the answer will be	**estimated estimating estimation**
even	not odd: level: equal	**evenly**
evening	the end of the day	
event	something that happens	
eventually	at last: in the end	
ever	always: at all times	
evergreen	staying green all the year	
every	each one	**everybody everyone everything everywhere**
evil	wicked	
ewe	a female sheep	
exact	correct	**exactly**
exaggerate	to make something seem more than it is	**exaggerated exaggerating exaggeration**
examine	1. to look at carefully 2. to test	**examination examined examining**
example	a pattern: something to be copied	
excellent	very good indeed	
except	leaving out: but for	**exception**
exchange	1. a telephone switch-board 2. to change one thing for another	**exchanged exchanging**
excite	to thrill someone	**excited excitement exciting**

excursion	a pleasure trip	
excuse	1. a reason	**excused**
	2. to forgive	**excusing**
exercise	1. a practice	**exercised**
	2. to use your muscles by moving about	**exercising**
exhaust	1. the pipe that carries away waste fumes from an engine	**exhausted** **exhausting**
	2. to make tired	
exhibition	a display	
exist	to be	**existed** **existence** **existing**
exit	the way out	
expand	to get larger	**expanded** **expanding** **expanse**
expect	to look forward to	**expected** **expecting**
expedition	a journey by land or sea to discover things	
expel	to drive out: to turn out	**expelled** **expelling**
expense	the cost of something	**expensive**
experiment	a trial or a test	**experi- mental**
expert	someone who is very good in a certain job or subject	
explain	to make the meaning clear	**explained** **explaining** **explanation**
explode	to burst with a loud noise	**exploded** **exploding** **explosion** **explosive**
explore	to search	**exploration** **explored** **explorer** **exploring**
export	to send goods out of the country	**exported** **exporting**

express	1. a fast train	**expresses**
	2. to put into words or writing	**expressed**
		expresses
		expressing
extra	in addition	
extraordinary	out of the ordinary: very unusual	
eye	part of the head with which you see	**eyebrow**
		eyelash
		eyelid
		eyesight

f

fable	a story about animals, making them like real people	
face	1. the front part of your head	**faced**
	2. to turn your head towards	**facing**
fact	something that is true	
factor	a number that goes exactly into another number	**factorise**
factory	a building where things are made	**factories**
fade	1. to lose colour	**faded**
	2. to disappear slowly: to get weaker slowly	**fading**
fail	to try to do something and be unable to do it	**failed**
		failing
		failure
faint	1. not clear: dim: weak	**fainted**
	2. to lose your senses as if you were asleep	**fainting**
		faintly
fair	1. a collection of sideshows and roundabouts	**fairly**
	2. a big market	
	3. honest: just	
	4. beautiful	
	5. light-coloured	
	6. not very good	
	7. dry and sunny	

fairy	a small person in a story who does good by magic	**fairies** **fairyland** **fairytale**
faithful	trusting: reliable	**faithfully**
fake	something which is not what it is said to be	
fall	to tumble: to drop	**fallen** **falling** **fell**
false	1. not real 2. not true	
family	a group of people or things related to each other	**families**
famine	a very great shortage of food	
famished	very hungry	
famous	well known: important	
fancy	1. pretty: decorated 2. to imagine 3. to want	**fancied** **fancies** **fancying**
fare	the amount you pay to travel from one place to another	
farewell	goodbye	
farm	land which is tilled: land on which cattle are reared	**farmed** **farmhouse** **farming** **farmyard**
farmer	a person who looks after a farm	
farther	a longer way away	**farthest**
fast	1. quick: speedy 2. fixed tightly	**faster** **fastest**
fasten	1. to fix tightly 2. to join together	**fastened** **fastener** **fastening**
father	a male parent	
fault	1. a mistake 2. a failing	**faulty**
favour	a kindness	**favourite**
fawn	1. a yellowish-brown colour 2. a young deer	

fear	1. dread: terror 2. to be afraid of	**feared fearful fearing fearless fearlessly**
feast	a very special meal: a festival	**feasted feasting**
feather	(A bird's body is covered with *feathers*)	**feathered feathery**
February	the second month of the year	
fed	(She *fed* her canary on bird seed)	
feeble	weak. dim	
feed	1. to give food to 2. to eat	**fed feeding**
feel	1. to touch 2. to notice 3. to have feeling	**feeling felt**
feet	(John's shoes pinched his *feet*)	
fell	(Rain *fell* and the match was stopped)	
fellow	a man or a boy	
felt	1. a thick woollen cloth 2. (I *felt* ill, so I stayed at home)	
female	a woman or a girl	
fence	a barrier round a garden or field to keep people out or animals in	**fencing**
fender	a metal guard to keep coals from falling from the fireplace	
fern	a plant with no flowers, found in woods	
ferret	a small thin animal that clears rabbits out of their holes	
ferry	a boat that travels backwards and forwards over a narrow stretch of water	**ferries**
festival	a time for merry-making	

fetch	to go for something and bring it back	**fetched** **fetches** **fetching**
fever	an illness that makes you feel hot	**feverish**
fibre	a small thread of something	
fiction	a story that is made up	
fiddle	1. another word for violin	
	2. to play idly with something	**fiddled** **fiddling**
fidget	to move restlessly	**fidgeted** **fidgeting** **fidgety**
field	1. a piece of land with a hedge or fence round it	
	2. to catch, stop or throw the ball at cricket	**fielded** **fielder** **fielding**
fierce	savage: cruel	**fiercely**
fifteen	15	**fifteenth**
fifth	5th	
fifty	50	**fiftieth**
fight	1. a struggle	**fighting**
	2. to struggle with	**fought**
figure	a number	
file	1. a tool for smoothing things	**filed**
	2. a line of people one behind another	**filing**
	3. to use a file	
fill	to make full	**filled** **filling**
film	1. a moving picture shown on a screen	**filmed** **filming**
	2. a roll put in a camera for taking photographs	
	3. a thin skin	
	4. to take a moving picture of something	
filter	material for straining liquids	
filthy	dirty: foul	

final	the last: at the very end	**finalist** **finally**
find	to discover: to come across	**finding** **found**
fine	1. money to be paid as a punishment for something you have done wrong	**fined**
	2. sunny	**finer**
	3. thin	**finest**
	4. excellent	
finger	(I have four *fingers* and one thumb on each hand)	**finger-nail** **finger-print**
finish	to end: to complete	**finished** **finishes** **finishing**
fir	a tall evergreen tree	
fire	1. when something burns	**fired**
	2. to shoot with a gun	**firing**
firefighter	a person whose job it is to put out fires	
fireplace	the place in a room where the fire burns	
fireside	the place near a fire	
firewood	wood used for lighting a fire	
fireworks	(We let off *fireworks* on November 5th each year)	
firm	1. a business	
	2. strong: steady	**firmly**
first	at the beginning: with nothing in front	**firstly**
fish	1. one of a group of animals that live in water	fish or fishes
	2. to try to catch fish	**fished** **fishes** **fishing**
fisherman	someone who catches fish	fishermen
fishmonger	someone who sells fish	
fist	a tightly closed hand	

fit	1. healthy 2. to be the right size	**fitted** **fitter** **fittest** **fitting**
five	5	**fifth**
fix	1. trouble 2. to fasten 3. to arrange	 **fixed** **fixes** **fixing**
fixture	a match or game arranged against another team	
flag	a banner on a stick or pole	
flake	a small, thin, light piece	
flame	1. the blaze of a fire 2. to burn like a flame	**flamed** **flaming**
flannel	1. smooth cloth made of wool 2. face-cloth	
flap	to move like wings	**flapped** **flapping**
flare	to throw out flames suddenly	**flared** **flaring**
flash	1. a light that suddenly comes and goes 2. to come and go very quickly	**flashes** **flashed** **flashes** **flashing**
flask	a small bottle with a narrow neck	
flat	1. a set of rooms on one floor 2. level and smooth 3. below the note in music	 **flatter** **flattest**
flatten	to make flat	**flattened** **flattening**
flavour	1. the taste of anything 2. to make tasty	**flavoured** **flavouring**
flea	a tiny, jumping insect that bites	
fled	ran away	
fleet	a group of ships, lorries or buses	

flesh	the soft part of the body, under the skin	**fleshy**
flew	(The bird *flew* high into the air)	
flick	to hit something lightly	**flicked** **flicking**
flicker	to burn shakily	**flickered** **flickering**
flies	(An owl usually *flies* at night)	
flight	a journey by air	
fling	to throw hard	**flinging** **flung**
flint	a very hard kind of rock	
float	to rest on, or near, the top of water	**floated** **floating**
flock	a number of birds or animals together	
flood	1. an overflow of water from a river or the sea 2. to overfill with liquid	**flooded** **flooding** **floodlight**
floor	the part of a room on which you walk	
flour	corn ground to powder	
flow	to move along smoothly	**flowed** **flowing**
flower	a blossom on a plant	**flowery**
'flu	short way of writing influenza	
fluff	soft, feathery stuff	**fluffy**
flung	(He *flung* the ball at the wicket)	
flute	a musical wind instrument	
fly	1. a small winged insect 2. to move through the air	**flies** **flew** **flies** **flown** **flying**
foam	1. froth 2. to make foam	**foamed** **foaming**
foggy	very misty	**foggier** **foggiest**

fo

fold	1. a crease	**folded**
	2. a fenced area in which	**folding**
	sheep are kept	
	3. to crease: to bend over	
folder	a cover in which to keep papers	
follow	1. to come after: to go behind	**followed**
	2. to understand	**follower**
		following
fond	loving	**fondly**
food	anything to eat or drink	
fool	1. a very silly person	**fooled**
	2. to make someone believe	**fooling**
	something that is not true	**foolish**
		foolishly
foot	1. the lowest part of the leg	
	2. the lowest part of anything	
	3. a measure of length	
football	a winter game played with a large leather ball	**footballer**
footpath	a narrow path to walk on	
footprint	the mark left by a foot	
footstep	the sound of a step	
forbid	to tell someone that they must not do something	**forbade**
		forbidden
		forbidding
force	1. strength	
	2. to make someone do something against his will	**forced**
		forcing
forecast	to say what will happen	**forecasting**
forehead	the part of the head just above the eyes	
foreign	belonging to another land	**foreigner**
foreman	a supervisor in charge of some workers	**foremen**
forest	a large area of trees	
forget	1. to put out of your mind	**forgetful**
	2. not to be able to remember	**forgetting**
		forgot
		forgotten

forgive	to pardon: to stop being cross with someone	**forgave** **forgiven** **forgiveness** **forgiving**
fork	1. a pronged tool for lifting earth or food 2. where a road divides in two	**forked**
form	1. the shape 2. a class 3. a bench 4. questions on a paper with blank spaces for the answers 5. to make	**formed** **forming**
fort	a castle, or strong building, which can be defended	**fortress**
fortnight	two weeks	
fortune	1. luck 2. wealth	**fortunate** **fortunately**
forty	40	**fortieth**
forward	to the front: onwards	
fossil	the remains or print of an ancient animal or plant, found in rock	
fought	(The boxer *fought* hard, but was beaten)	
foul	1. dirty: filthy 2. not to keep to the rules of the game	**fouled** **fouling**
found	(I lost my watch but *found* it the next day)	
fountain	a jet of water shooting up-wards	
four	4	**fourth**
fourteen	14	**fourteenth**
fowl	a cock or hen	**fowl**
fox	a sly, wild animal like a dog	**foxes**
fraction	a part of anything	
frame	1. the border round a picture 2. the supports around which something is built	

fr

freckle	a small brown spot on the skin	**freckled**
free	1. able to do as you like 2. loose 3. not costing anything	**freed** **freeing** **freely**
freedom	being free	
freeze	1. to turn water into ice 2. to be very cold	**freezing** **froze** **frozen**
fresh	1. new 2. clean and pure 3. not feeling tired	**freshly**
Friday	the sixth day of the week	
fried	(My father *fried* the fish)	
friend	someone you are fond of	**friendly** **friendship**
frieze	a border or strip of pictures on a wall	
fright	fear: terror	**frighten** **frightened** **frightening** **frightful**
frill	a wavy edge on anything	**frilled** **frilly**
fringe	short hair combed down over the forehead	
frisky	lively	
frock	a dress	
frog	a small animal that jumps and lives in and out of water	
from	out of	
front	the forward part	
frost	frozen dew or mist	**frosty**
froth	lots of air bubbles on top of a liquid	**frothed** **frothing** **frothy**
frown	to draw the eye-brows together	**frowned** **frowning**

frozen	1. turned to ice	
	2. stiff with cold	
fruit	the part of a plant which is sometimes eaten and which has seeds inside	
fry	to cook in boiling fat or oil	**fried** **fries** **frying**
fuel	anything used to make heat or power	
full	filled so that no more can go in	**fully**
fumble	to be clumsy in handling something	**fumbled** **fumbling**
fumes	smoke, gas or steam	
fund	money collected for a special reason	
funeral	a burial service	
funnel	1. the chimney of a ship	
	2. a tube with a wide mouth for pouring liquids	
funny	comical	**funnier** **funniest**
fur	the hair and skin of an animal	**furry**
furnace	a closed fireplace where a very hot fire can be made	
furnish	to fit up a house with tables, chairs, beds and other things	**furnished** **furnishes** **furnishing** **furniture**
furrow	a trench made by a plough	
further	1. a longer way away	**furthest**
	2. more	
	3. in addition	
fury	anger: rage	**furious** **furiously**
fuse	a safety wire that melts if the electric wires joined to it become too hot	**fused** **fusing**
fuselage	the body of an aircraft	

fuss	to worry about things that do not matter	**fussy**
future	the time which has yet to come	

g

gag	1. something put over some-one's mouth so that he can-not talk 2. to stop up someone's mouth	**gagged** **gagging**
gaily	merrily: happily	
gain	to get: obtain	**gained** **gaining**
gale	a very strong wind	
gallon	eight pints	
gallop	to run in leaps, as a horse does	**galloped** **galloping**
game	1. a sport 2. animals or birds that are hunted	
gander	a male goose	
gang	a group of people who work together	**gangster**
garage	a place where cars are re-paired or where they are kept	
garden	land used for growing flowers, fruit and vegetables	**gardener** **gardening**
gas	1. a fuel 2. anything, such as air, which is neither solid nor liquid	
gate	a door in a fence or wall	
gather	to collect together	**gathered** **gathering**
gave	(Sarah *gave* her sister some of her marbles)	

gaze	to stare at	**gazed**
		gazing
gazelle	a small antelope	
geese	the plural of goose	
general	1. a very important officer in the army	
	2. usual	**generally**
generous	not mean: ready to help anyone	**generously**
gentle	quiet: kind	**gently**
gentleman	a man who is well-mannered	gentlemen
geography	the study of people, places and things	
germ	a living thing which is too small to be seen without a magnifying glass but which may make you ill	
get	1. to obtain: to receive	**getting**
	2. to become	**got**
ghost	1. something imagined but not real	**ghostly**
	2. the soul of a person who is dead	
giant	a very large person or thing	
giddy	dizzy	**giddier**
		giddiest
		giddiness
gift	a present: something given	
ginger	1. a reddish-yellow colour	
	2. the root of a plant which tastes very hot	**gingerbread**
gipsy	one of a type of dark-skinned people who wander from place to place	gipsies
giraffe	an animal with very long legs and neck	
girl	a female child	
give	to hand over something	**gave**
		given
		giving

glacier	a slow-moving river of ice	
glad	pleased	**gladly**
glance	1. a quick look	**glanced**
	2. to look quickly at something	**glancing**
glance off	to bounce off	
glare	1. to stare fiercely	**glared**
	2. to shine brightly and dazzle	**glaring**
glass	1. the stuff from which window-panes are made	
	2. a drinking cup made of glass	**glasses**
	3. a mirror	
glasses	a pair of spectacles	
glide	to move smoothly and quietly	**glided** **gliding**
glider	an aeroplane with no engine	
glimpse	a quick look at something	
glitter	to sparkle	**glittered** **glittering**
globe	1. a ball-shape	
	2. a map of the earth in the shape of a ball	
gloomy	1. dark	
	2. miserable	
glorious	splendid: magnificent	
glove	a covering for the hand	
glow	to burn brightly without flames	**glowed** **glowing**
glue	sticky stuff for joining things together	
glum	sad: gloomy	
gnat	a small mosquito or fly that bites	
gnaw	to keep biting something and so wear it away	**gnawed** **gnawing**
gnome	a dwarf who is supposed to live under the ground	

go	to move	goes going gone
goal	1. something to be aimed at 2. a target in a game	goalkeeper goalmouth goalpost
goat	a small animal with horns which is useful for its milk and hair	
gobble	to eat quickly and noisily	gobbled gobbling
goblin	an ugly elf who is full of mischief	
god	one who is worshipped	
godfather	a man who makes promises for a baby at its christening	
godmother	a woman who makes promises for a baby at its christening	
godparent	a godfather or godmother	
going	(We are *going* to the seaside in the summer)	
gold	a precious yellow metal	golden
gone	(My friend has *gone* away)	
good	1. well-behaved 2. above average 3. suitable	goodness
goodbye	(Before leaving we said *goodbye*)	
goose	a large bird with a long neck and webbed feet	geese
gooseberry	a small hairy green fruit	gooseberries
gorge	a narrow strip of land with cliffs or mountains on either side	
gorgeous	beautifully coloured	
gorilla	the largest kind of ape	

gorse	a prickly bush with yellow flowers	
govern	to rule over	**governed** **governing** **government** **governor**
grab	to snatch	**grabbed** **grabbing**
grace	1. charm: beauty 2. a prayer before or after meals	**gracious**
graceful	full of charm: moving beautifully and easily	**gracefully**
gradually	little by little	
grain	1. corn 2. a very small piece of anything 3. the pattern in a piece of wood	
gramophone	a machine that plays records, an old-fashioned record-player	
gramme	a measure of mass (weight) in the metric system	
grand	splendid: important	
grandchild	the child of a person's son or daughter	**grandchildren**
grandfather	the father of a person's mother or father	
grandmother	the mother of a person's mother or father	
grandson	the son of a person's son or daughter	
granite	a very hard rock	
granny	grandmother	**grannies**
grape	the fruit of the vine plant	
grapefruit	a pale yellow fruit like a large orange	
graph	a diagram giving mathematical information, usually drawn on squared paper	

grasp	1. a firm grip 2. to take hold of	**grasped** **grasping**
grass	plants with thin green leaves grown as lawns and in fields	grass or grasses
grasshopper	a small jumping insect	
grate	a part of a fireplace	
grateful	thankful	**gratefully**
grave	1. a burial place 2. solemn: serious	**gravely** **gravestone** **graveyard**
gravity	the force that pulls things towards the centre of the earth	
gravy	the juice that comes from meat when it is cooked	
graze	1. to feed on grass in a field 2. to scrape the skin	**grazed** **grazing**
grease	1. thick fat or oil 2. to put grease on something	**greased** **greasing** **greasy**
great	large: important	**greater** **greatest** **greatly**
greedy	wanting more than is good for you	**greedier** **greediest** **greedily** **greediness**
green	the colour of grass	
greengrocer	someone who sells fruit and vegetables	
greenhouse	a glass house for plants	
greet	to welcome	**greeted** **greeting**
grew	(The seed *grew* into a beautiful plant)	
grey	the colour of a rainy sky	**greyish**
greyhound	a long-legged dog that runs very fast	
grin	1. a broad smile 2. to give a broad smile	**grinned** **grinning**

grind	1. to crush to powder 2. to sharpen	grinding ground
grip	1. a tight hold 2. to hold tightly	gripped gripping
gristle	the tough, stringy part of meat	gristly
grit	small bits of sand or stone	gritty
groan	1. a deep, slow sound made in pain, or when you are sad 2. to moan in pain or sadness	groaned groaning
grocer	someone who sells most kinds of dry or tinned foods	
grocery	what you buy from the grocer	groceries
ground	1. the earth 2. crushed to powder	
group	a number of people or things	
grouse	1. a moorland bird 2. a grumble 3. to complain or grumble	grouse groused grousing
grow	1. to get larger 2. to produce 3. to become	grew growing grown growth
growl	the sound a dog makes when it is disturbed	growled growling
grub	a caterpillar or a maggot	
grubby	dirty and untidy	
grumble	to complain	grumbled grumbling
grunt	to make a short pig-like noise	grunted grunting
guard	to look after: to keep safe	guarded guarding
guess	to say something without being sure	guessed guesses guessing
guide	1. a person who shows the way 2. to show the way	guided guiding

guilty	having done something wrong
guinea-pig	a small animal kept as a pet
guitar	a musical instrument with six strings
gum	1. the part of your mouth in which your teeth grow 2. a thick liquid for sticking **gummed** things together **gumming** 3. to stick with gum
gunpowder	powder used for blowing things up
gust	a sudden rush of wind **gusty**
gutter	the edge of a road or roof along which water can run away
guy	a doll dressed up and meant to be like Guy Fawkes
gymnasium	a room for physical training
gypsy	one of a type of people who **gypsies** travel from place to place

h

habit	custom: anything you do regu- **habitual** larly
haddock	a fish which belongs to the **haddock** cod family of fish
hail	frozen rain
hair	it grows on people's heads **hair-cut** and on some animals' bodies **hairdresser** **hairy**
half	one of the parts of something **halves** divided in two
halfpenny	two of them make one penny **halfpennies**

hall	1. a large room in a building where people can gather together 2. the front passage in a house	
halo	a ring of light	**haloes**
halt	to come to a stop	**halted** **halting**
halve	to divide into two parts, both the same size	**halved** **halves** **halving**
hammer	1. a tool with a heavy head for knocking things 2. to use a hammer	**hammered** **hammering**
hamster	an animal like a large mouse	
hand	1. the part of the body at the end of the arm 2. to pass something to someone	**handed** **handful** **handing**
handcuffs	a pair of steel rings put round a prisoner's wrists	
handkerchief	a piece of cloth for wiping your nose	
handle	1. the part of anything for holding 2. to hold with your hands	**handled** **handling**
handle-bar	the bar across a bicycle which you hold to guide it	
handsome	good-looking	
handwriting	words written by hand	
handy	1. useful 2. nearby 3. clever with your hands	**handier** **handiest**
hang	to fasten anything so that it can swing	**hanged** **hanging** **hung**
hangar	a shed for aeroplanes	
happen	to take place	**happened** **happening**

happy	pleased: joyful	**happier** **happiest** **happily** **happiness**
harbour	a place where ships can shelter	
hard	1. tough and solid 2. difficult 3. strict	
hardly	only just	
hare	an animal that is like a large rabbit	
harm	1. damage: hurt 2. to damage or hurt	**harmed** **harmful** **harming**
harpoon	a spear for killing whales	
harvest	1. crops gathered in 2. the time for gathering in crops 3. to gather in crops	**harvested** **harvester** **harvesting**
haste	hurry: speed	**hasten** **hasty**
hat	a covering for the head	
hatch	1. an opening in a wall, floor, roof or ship's deck 2. to be born from an egg	**hatches** **hatched** **hatches** **hatching** **hatchway**
hate	to dislike a great deal	**hated** **hateful** **hating** **hatred**
haunted	visited by ghosts	
have	to own: to hold	**had** **having**
hayrick **haystack**	a large neat pile of hay	
haze	a light mist	**hazy**
hazel	a small tree which sometimes produces nuts	

head	1. the top of the body 2. the top part of anything 3. the most important 4. to knock a ball with your head	**headed** **headfirst** **heading** **head-** **quarters**
headache	a pain in the head	
headlight	one of the main lights on the front of a car	
headlong	rashly, without thought	
headmaster	the chief master in a school	
headmistress	the chief mistress in a school	**head-** **mistresses**
heal	to cure: to get better	**healed** **healing**
health	the state your body is in when it is fit	**healthier** **healthiest** **healthy**
heap	1. a pile 2. to pile things up	**heaped** **heaping**
hear	to listen to, or get word from someone	**heard** **hearing**
heart	1. the part of the body that pumps blood 2. the centre of anything	**heartbeat** **heartfelt** **hearty**
heat	1. warmth 2. to warm anything	**heated** **heating**
heath	moorland: waste land with grass and heather growing on it	
heather	a plant that grows on heaths	
heaven	the kingdom of God	**heavenly**
heavy	having a lot of mass (weight)	**heavier** **heaviest** **heavily**
hedge	a border made of shrubs or bushes which acts as a fence	
hedgehog	a small animal with a prickly back	

heel	the back part of the foot or shoe	**heeled**
heel over	to tilt: to lean	
height	how tall a thing is	
held	(The guard *held* up her flag)	
helicopter	an aircraft that has a pro-peller on the top and can fly straight upwards	
helmet	a very strong covering to pro-tect the head	
help	1. assistance: aid 2. to assist: to aid	**helped** **helpful** **helpfully** **helping** **helpless** **helplessly**
hem	1. the edge of a piece of cloth turned over and stitched 2. to turn over and stitch the edge of a piece of cloth	**hemmed** **hemming**
herd	a number of animals together	
here	in this place	
hero	a very brave man or boy	**heroes** **heroic**
heroine	a very brave woman or girl	
herring	a small sea fish caught for food	
herself	she	
hesitate	to wait for a moment before doing something	**hesitated** **hesitating** **hesitation**
hexagon	a flat shape with six sides	
hibernate	to sleep all through the winter	**hibernated** **hibernating** **hibernation**
hide	1. the skin of an animal 2. to put out of sight	**hid** **hidden** **hiding**

high	tall: far up	**higher** **highest** **highly**
highway	a road	
highwayman	a highway robber	highwaymen
hi-jack	to force a pilot of an aircraft to change course	**hi-jacked** **hi-jacking**
hike	to walk a long distance, usually on holiday	**hiked** **hiker** **hiking**
hill	a small mountain	**hilly**
himself	he	
hinder	to delay or prevent	**hindered** **hindering** **hindrance**
hinge	a joint on which a door or lid swings	
hippopotamus	a large, heavy animal that lives in water and on land	hippopota- muses
hire	to pay for the use of something	**hired** **hiring**
history	the subject that tells of people or things of the past	**historical**
hitch-hike	to ask for a free lift in a car or lorry	**hitch-hiked** **hitch-hiking**
hive	a home for bees making honey	
hoard	1. a store of things hidden away 2. to store things up in secret	**hoarded** **hoarding**
hoarse	rough sounding: husky	
hobble	to walk awkwardly, as when you are lame	**hobbled** **hobbling**
hobby	a pastime	hobbies
hockey	a game played with bent sticks and a small ball	
hold	1. the part of the ship where the cargo is stored 2. to take in your hands 3. to contain	**held** **holder** **holding**

hole	an opening: a hollow	
holiday	a time for doing what you like	
hollow	1. a hole 2. empty	
holly	an evergreen bush with red berries and prickly leaves	
hollyhock	a tall plant with large flowers	
holster	a holder for a revolver	
holy	pure: without sin	**holier** **holiest** **holiness**
home	where anyone lives	**homeless** **homely** **homesick** **homeward** **homework**
honest	truthful	**honestly** **honesty**
honey	the sweet syrup that bees make	
honeysuckle	a climbing plant with a sweet-smelling flower	
honour	1. glory 2. to praise or respect	**honoured** **honouring**
hood	a covering for the head and neck	**hooded**
hoof	the bottom part of some animal's feet	**hooves**
hook	a curved piece of metal	**hooked** **hooking**
hooligan	a rough, badly-behaved person	
hoop	a large wooden or metal ring	
hoot	to make a sound like an owl	**hooted** **hooter** **hooting**
hop	1. a plant used for making beer 2. to jump along on one foot	**hopped** **hopping**

hope	to wish for something to come true	**hoped** **hopeful** **hopefully** **hopeless** **hopelessly** **hoping**
horizon	where the sky seems to meet the land	**horizontal**
horn	1. a curved bone covered with hard skin sticking out of an animal's head 2. a musical wind instrument	
horrible	awful: dreadful	**horribly**
horrid	frightful: horrible	**horridly**
horrified	shocked	
horror	dread: great fear	
horse	a large animal used for riding or pulling loads	**horseshoe**
hose	a long rubber or plastic pipe	**hosepipe**
hospital	a building where sick people are looked after	
hot	very warm	**hotly** **hotter** **hottest**
hotel	a place where people pay to sleep and eat	
hound	a dog used in hunting	
hour	sixty minutes	**hourly**
house	a building in which a family lives	**household** **housekeeper** **housekeep-ing** **housing**
hover	to stay in the air over a place	
hovercraft	a cross between a ship and an aircraft, which hovers just above the surface	**hovercraft**
howl	1. a long, loud cry, like that of a dog 2. to cry out like a dog	**howled** **howling**

huddle	to get close together	**huddled** **huddling**
hug	to put your arms round	**hugged** **hugging**
huge	very large	
hum	to make a sound like a bee	**hummed** **humming**
hump	a lump on the back	**humped**
hundred	100	**hundredth**
hundredweight	one hundred and twelve pounds	
hung	(Jim *hung* his cap on the peg)	
hunger	the need for food	**hungrier** **hungriest** **hungrily** **hungry**
hunt	to try to catch wild animals	**hunted** **hunting**
hunt for	to search for	**hunter** **hunting** **huntsman**
hurrah	a shout of joy	
hurricane	a very strong wind	
hurry	to go quickly	**hurried** **hurries** **hurrying**
hurt	to harm: to damage	**hurting**
husband	a man who has a wife	
hush	silence	
hutch	a cage for rabbits	**hutches**
hyacinth	a sweet-smelling spring flower	
hyena	a wild animal like a dog, that lives in Africa or Asia	
hymn	a song of praise	

i

ice	frozen water	**iceberg** **ice-cream** **iced** **icing** **icy**
icicle	ice that hangs like a spike	
idea	a thought	
idiot	a fool	
idle	doing nothing	**idled** **idleness** **idling** **idly**
igloo	an Inuit ice-house	
ill	1. not well 2. evil	**illness**
imagine	to make a picture of something in your mind	**imagination** **imagined** **imagining**
imitate	to do the same as someone else	**imitated** **imitating** **imitation**
immediately	straight away	
impatient	not willing to wait: restless	**impatience**
import	to bring goods into the country	**imported** **importing**
important	worth thinking about or looking at	**importance**
impossible	cannot be done	**impossibility**
improve	to make, or to get, better	**improved** **improve- ment** **improving**
inch	twelve of them make a foot	inches
include	to put with other things in a a group	**included** **including**
increase	1. to get bigger 2. to make bigger	**increased** **increasing**

indeed	really	
index	alphabetical list showing where to find things in a book	indexes indices
indoors	in a house or building	
infant	a very young child	
influenza	a feverish cold	
inform	to tell someone about something	information informed informing
injure	to hurt in some way	injured injuring injury
ink	used with a pen for writing	inkwell inky
inland	away from the sea	
innings	the time spent batting by a team or one player	
innocent	not guilty	
inquire	to ask about	inquired inquiring inquiry
insect	a small creature	
inside	within	
insist	to be very firm in saying something	insisted insisting
insolent	rude: cheeky	insolence
inspect	to look at closely for faults	inspected inspecting inspection inspector
instalment	one part of a story or payment	
instant	a very short space of time	instantly
instead	in place of	
instrument	1. a special tool 2. anything with which music is made	
intelligent	quick at learning	intelligence
intend	to be going to do something	intended intending intention

interest	1. curiosity	**interested**
	2. what people charge you if	**interesting**
	they lend you money	
	3. to hold your attention	
interfere	1. to meddle	**interfered**
	2. to get in the way	**interference**
		interfering
interrupt	to stop someone when he is	**interrupted**
	talking or working	**interrupting**
		interruption
interval	1. the space between	
	2. a rest	
into	right in	
introduce	1. to bring in	**introduced**
	2. to bring two people to-	**introducing**
	gether	**introduction**
invade	to enter another country in	**invaded**
	order to conquer it	**invading**
		invasion
invalid	a person who is not well	
invent	to make for the first time	**invented**
		inventing
		invention
		inventor
investigate	to examine very carefully	**investigated**
		investigat-
		ing
		investiga-
		tion
invisible	unable to be seen	
invite	to ask someone to come	**invitation**
		invited
		inviting
iron	1. a hard metal	
	2. a tool for smoothing cloth	**ironed**
	3. to smooth with an iron	**ironing**
ironmonger	a person who sells iron goods	
island	land surrounded by water	
isosceles	a triangle with two of its sides	
	equal is called an isosceles	
	triangle	

itch	1. a tickling on your skin	**itches**
	2. to feel a tickling on your skin	**itched**
		itches
		itching
itself	it	
ivory	the material elephants' tusks are made of	
ivy	an evergreen climbing plant	

j

jab	to poke in a rough way	**jabbed**
		jabbing
jack	a tool for raising heavy things	
jackal	a wild animal like a dog	
jackdaw	the smallest bird of the crow family	
jacket	a short coat	
jagged	rough at the edge	
jaguar	a fast-running wild animal	
jail	1. a prison	**jailer**
	2. to put a person in prison	
jam	1. fruit boiled with sugar	
	2. to become packed tightly	**jammed**
		jamming
January	the first month of the year	
jaw	the lower part of the face	
jazz	lively music with a strong rhythm	
jealous	envious	**jealousy**
jeans	tight trousers made from a material like thin canvas	
jeep	a small truck which can travel over rough ground and which has a very powerful engine	
jelly	fruit or meat juice that has set stiff	**jellies**

jellyfish	a fish like a floating piece of jelly	jellyfish or jellyfishes
jerk	to move something suddenly	**jerked jerking jerky**
jersey	a long-sleeved pullover	
jet	a thin stream of liquid or gas forced out through a pipe	**jet-propelled**
jetty	a small pier	**jetties**
jewel	a precious stone	**jewelled jeweller jewellery**
jig-saw	a picture cut into pieces that can be fitted together	
job	the work a person does	
jockey	a person who rides racehorses	
jog	1. to push with the elbow or hand 2. to trot in a tired way	**jogged jogging**
join	1. to fix things together 2. to become a member of	**joined joining**
joint	1. a piece of meat 2. a place where parts of something are joined	**jointed**
joke	1. something said or done that is funny 2. to make a joke	**joked joker joking**
jolly	happy: merry	**jollier jolliest**
journalist	someone who writes for a newspaper or magazine	
journey	going from one place to another	
joy	happiness: gladness	**joyful joyfully**
judge	1. someone who hears both sides of an argument, and then decides which is right 2. to decide: to give an opinion about something	**judged judgement judging**

juggler	a person who does throwing and catching tricks	
juice	the liquid from fruit	**juicy**
July	the seventh month of the year	
jumble	1. a number of things mixed up 2. to mix up	**jumbled** **jumbling**
jump	to spring: to leap	**jumped** **jumping**
jumper	a blouse made of wool	
June	the sixth month of the year	
jungle	a forest of thickly twined trees, plants and bushes, in hot lands	
junior	a younger person: younger	
junk	1. rubbish 2. a Chinese sailing boat	
jury	a group of people who decide whether someone is guilty or not	**juries**
just	1. fair 2. exactly: at this very minute	
justice	fairness	

k

kangaroo	an Australian animal with long back legs, which moves by jumping	
kayak	an Inuit canoe	
keel	a length of wood or metal on which a boat is built, and which stops it turning over	
keen	1. eager 2. sharp	**keener** **keenest** **keenly**

keep	1. part of a castle	
	2. to take care of	**keeper**
	3. to own something	**keeping**
	4. to stay fresh	**kept**
	5. to continue	
kennel	a house for a dog	
kept	(He *kept* his coat on because it was cold)	
kerb	the stone edge of a path or pavement	**kerbstone**
ketchup	sauce made from vegetables	
kettle	a container made of metal, used for boiling water	
key	1. used for locking and unlocking doors	**keyhole**
	2. a thing on a piano or typewriter which is pressed down by the fingers	**keyboard**
kick	to hit with the foot	**kicked**
		kicking
kidnap	to steal a person, usually a child	**kidnapped**
		kidnapper
		kidnapping
kill	to take life	**killed**
		killer
		killing
kilogramme	a measure of mass (weight) in the metric system	
kilometre	a measure of length in the metric system	
kilt	a short skirt with a pattern of crossing stripes	
kind	1. a sort	**kinder**
	2. friendly: helpful	**kindest**
		kindhearted
		kindly
		kindness
king	the head man of a country	
kingdom	a country with a king or queen	
kipper	a herring dried over smoke	

kiss	1. a touch with the lips as a sign of love 2. to give a kiss	**kisses** **kissed** **kisses** **kissing**
kitchen	the room where food is prepared	
kite	a light frame covered with paper or cloth that flies in the air at the end of a string	
kitten	a young cat	
knee	the joint in the middle of the leg	
kneel	to go down on one or both knees	**kneeled** **kneeler** **kneeling** **knelt**
knew	(Jill *knew* the answer to the question)	
knife	a blade on a handle, used for cutting	**knives**
knight	one of the king's noblemen	
knit	to weave with needles	**knitted** **knitter** **knitting**
knob	a rounded door handle	**knobbly**
knock	1. to make a sharp tap 2. to hit	**knocked** **knocker** **knocking**
knot	1. where string or rope is tied 2. to make a knot 3. a speed: one sea mile per hour	**knotted** **knotting**
know	1. to understand 2. to recognise	**knew** **knowing** **knowledge** **known**
knuckle	a joint in the fingers	

l

label	1. a slip of paper on something to say what it is or where it is going 2. to put a label on	**labelled** **labelling**
laboratory	a place where scientific experiments are done	**laboratories**
labour	work	**labourer**
lace	1. a fancy net material made from woven thread 2. a piece of cord for tying 3. to tie up with a lace	**laced** **lacing** **shoelace**
lad	a boy	
ladder	a set of steps which can be moved	
ladle	a large spoon with a long handle	
lady	1. a woman 2. the wife of a nobleman	**ladies**
lady-bird	a small beetle that flies	
lag	to go slowly and not to keep up	**lagged** **lagging**
lagoon	a shallow lake of sea water	
laid	(The hen *laid* an egg)	
lair	place where a wild animal lives or hides	
lake	a stretch of water inland	
lamb	a young sheep	
lame	crippled: not able to walk properly	**lamely**
lamp	a light, usually covered by glass	**lamp-post**
land	1. the ground 2. to come on land or shore from an aeroplane or ship	**landed** **landing** **landslide**
landing	the flat space at the top of the stairs	

landlady	a lady who keeps a boarding house or inn, or who owns a house that is rented	landladies
landlord	a man who keeps an inn or boarding house, or who owns a house that is rented	
lane	a narrow road or pathway	
language	words used by people of a country	
lanky	tall and thin	
lantern	a case with glass sides, into which a light is put	
lap	1. the top part of the legs of someone sitting down 2. once round a race track 3. to drink like a cat	**lapped** **lapping**
larch	a large tree with cones	larches
lard	fat from pigs, used for cooking	
larder	a cool room or cupboard for storing food	
large	big: great	**enlarge** **largely** **larger** **largest**
lark	a bird that sings sweetly and flies very high	
lash	1 a hair on the eye lid 2. to bind tightly, usually with a rope 3. to whip fiercely	lashes **lashed** **lashes** **lashing**
lass	a girl	lasses
lasso	a long rope with a loop at the end used by cowboys	lassoes
last	1. the shape of a foot, used by cobblers 2. after all the rest: at the end 3. to keep going on	**lasted** **lasting**
latch	a catch on a door or gate	latches
late	behind time	**lately** **later** **latest**

lather	froth made when soap and water are well mixed	**lathered** **lathering**
laugh	1. a sound made when you are happy or amused 2. to show you are amused	**laughed** **laughing** **laughter**
launch	1. a small boat 2. to slide a boat into water	**launches** **launched** **launches** **launching**
laundry	a building where clothes are washed, dried and ironed	**laundries**
lava	molten rocks from a volcano	
lavatory	a toilet	**lavatories**
lavender	a plant that is very sweet-smelling	
law	a rule which must be obeyed	**lawful** **lawless** **unlawful**
lawn	ground covered with short grass in a garden or park	**lawn-** **mower**
lawyer	someone who knows a great deal about laws	
lay	1. to produce an egg 2. to set 3. (Yesterday I *lay* in the sun all day)	**laid** **laying**
lazy	idle: not wanting to work	**lazier** **laziest** **laziness**
lead	1. a heavy grey metal 2. a piece of thin leather used as a rein for a dog 3. to show the way 4. to be in first place	**leader** **leading** **led**
leaf	1. the green, flat part of a plant or tree 2. a sheet of paper in a book	**leaves** **leaflet** **leafy**
league	1. a group of teams that play each other 2. an old measure of distance	

leak	1. a crack or hole through which liquid can run in or out 2. to let water in or out	**leaked** **leaking** **leaky**
lean	1. thin 2. without fat 3. to slope	**leaned** **leaning** **leant**
leap	to jump	**leaped** **leaping** **leapt**
learn	to get to know something	**learned** **learner** **learning** **learnt**
least	the smallest	
leather	the skin of some animals prepared for use	**leathery**
leave	1. to go away from 2. to allow to stay	**leaving** **left**
led	(Our team *led* all the way)	
ledge	a narrow shelf	
leek	a vegetable like a long onion	
left	1. gone away 2. the opposite side to the right	
legend	an ancient story	
lemon	a sour yellow fruit	**lemonade**
lend	to let someone use something belonging to you	**lending** **lent**
length	how long something is from one end to the other	
lengthen	to make longer	**lengthened** **lengthening**
lens	a circular piece of glass for bending light	**lenses**
Lent	the six weeks before Easter	
lent	(John *lent* me his book so that I could read it)	
leopard	a fierce animal with spotted fur	

less	not as much, or as many, as	
lesson	1. something you learn 2. the time spent in school on one subject at a time	
let	to allow	**letting**
letter	1. a written message sent to someone 2. the written shape of a sound; a part of the alphabet	
lettuce	a green-leaved plant used in salads	
level	1. flat or even 2. to flatten or to even up	**level-crossing** **levelled** **levelling**
lever	a rod or bar for lifting or moving things	
liar	someone who does not tell the truth	
library	1. a large number of books 2. a place where books are kept	**libraries**
licence	a form which gives you permission to do something	
lick	to touch with your tongue	**licked** **licking**
lie	1. an untruth 2. to say things which are untrue 3. to rest on your back or side	**lay** **lied** **lying**
life	1. the time from when you are born till when you die 2. being alive	**lives** **lifeless** **lifelike** **lifetime**
lift	1. a machine that takes you from floor to floor to save you using the stairs 2. to raise up	**lifted** **lifting**
lift-off	the moment when a space ship leaves the ground	

light	1. brightness 2. of little mass (weight) 3. to set on fire	**lighten** **lighter** **lightest** **lighting** **lightly** **lit**
lighthouse	a tower with a warning light for ships to see	
lightning	flashes of light in a thunderstorm	
like	1. the same or nearly the same as 2. to be fond of	**liked** **likely** **likeness**
lilac	1. a bush with white or mauve flowers 2. a mauve colour	
lily	a large flower with a long stem	**lilies**
limb	an arm or a leg	
limit	boundary: the edge: the furthest you are allowed to go	
limp	1. the uneven walk of a lame person 2. drooping 3. to walk unevenly	**limped** **limping**
limpet	a shell-fish that sticks firmly to rocks	
line	1. a long, thin mark 2. a row 3. to cover the inside of a thing	**lined** **lining**
line up	to form a row	
linen	cloth made from flax	
liner	a large ship for carrying people	
link	1. one part of a chain 2. to join two things together	**linked** **linking**
linoleum	a material for covering floors	
lint	a soft cloth for putting on cuts	
lion	a large, fierce wild animal	**lioness**

liquid	anything that flows like water	
liquorice	a root used for making sweets	
lisp	to sound 's' and 'z' like 'th'	**lisped** **lisping**
list	a number of things written one under the other	
listen	to hear carefully	**listened** **listener** **listening**
lit	(Mother *lit* the fire to make us warm)	
litre	a measure of capacity in the metric system	
litter	1. rubbish or waste paper left lying about 2. a number of animals born at the same time 3. a kind of stretcher	
little	small	
live	to be alive	**lived** **living**
lively	full of life	**livelier** **liveliest**
lizard	a small reptile with short legs and a tail	
load	1. something to be carried 2. to put things on to something to be carried	**loaded** **loading**
loaf	bread baked in a shape	**loaves**
loan	1. something that is lent 2. to lend	**loaned** **loaning**
lobster	a shell-fish which has two big claws	
local	to do with a place or district	
loch	Scottish word for lake	
lock	1. a fastening which is opened or closed with a key 2. to fasten by turning the key in a lock	**locked** **locker** **locking**
locomotive	a railway engine	

lodge	1. a small house at the gates of a large house or castle 2. to live with for a time	**lodged** **lodger** **lodging**
loft	a store-room in a roof	**lofty**
lollipop	a sweet on a stick	
lonely	1. without friends 2. with no-one near	**lonelier** **loneliest** **loneliness**
long	of some length	**longer** **longest**
long for	to want something very much	**longed** **longing**
look	1. to turn one's eyes towards 2. to seem to be	**looked** **looking**
look for	to seek	
loom	1. a frame on which wool or cotton thread is woven 2. to appear gradually, as in a fog	**loomed** **looming**
loop	1. a ring made with wire, string or thread 2. to form a loop	**looped** **looping**
loose	1. free to move 2. to set free	**loosely** **loosen** **loosened** **loosening** **looser** **loosest**
lord	a nobleman	**lordship**
lorry	a motor truck for carrying loads	**lorries**
lose	1. to be unable to find something 2. to be beaten in a game	**loser** **losing** **lost**
loss	anything you lose	**losses**
loud	making a lot of noise	**louder** **loudest** **loudly** **loud- 　speaker**

lounge	a sitting-room	
love	1. goodness	lovable
	2. to be fond of	loved
		loving
		lovingly
lovely	beautiful: very pleasing	lovelier
		loveliest
		loveliness
low	not high or tall	lower
		lowest
luck	1. chance	luckier
	2. good fortune	luckiest
		luckily
		lucky
luggage	a traveller's baggage	
lukewarm	1. slightly warm	
	2. half-hearted	
lullaby	a song to help a baby go to sleep	lullabies
lumberjack	a person who cuts down trees for a living	
lump	1. a shapeless piece of any-thing	
	2. a swelling	
lunar	to do with the moon	
lunar module	the part of a space ship used for landing on the moon	
lunatic	a mad person	
lunch	a meal eaten in the middle of the day	lunches
lungs	the part of the body inside the chest where you breathe air	
lurk	to hide, in order to lie in wait	lurked
		lurking
luxury	something pleasant but not necessary	luxuries
lying	1. not telling the truth	
	2. (Daisy was *lying* on her bed)	
lynx	a kind of wild cat	lynxes

m

macaroni	tubes made from a wheat paste which become soft when they are cooked	
machine	something constructed, with moving parts, which helps to do work	
mackerel	a sea fish whose oily flesh is good to eat	mackerel
mackintosh	a raincoat	mackin- toshes
made	(Mary's mother *made* her a new dress)	
magazine	a book or paper that comes out regularly	
magic	1. when impossible things seem to come true 2. conjuring tricks	magical
magician	a person who does things which seem impossible	
magnet	a bar of iron to which some other metals will cling	magnetised magnetising
magnificent	splendid: grand to look at	
magnify	1. to make something seem bigger than it is by using a magnifying glass 2. to exaggerate	magnified magnifies magnifying
magpie	a black and white bird with a long tail	
maid	1. a young girl 2. a woman servant	
mail	anything sent by post	
main	most important	mainly
majesty	a title for a king or queen	majesties
make	1. to build or fit together 2. to force	made maker making

make up   to invent

male   a man or a boy

mammal   an animal, such as a dog or human, which has warm blood and feeds its young at the breast

manage
1. to be in charge of something
2. just to be able to do something

managed
manager
managing

mane   the long hair on the neck of a horse or lion

mangle
1. a machine which presses the water out of washing
2. to use a mangle

mangled
mangling

manner
1. the way someone behaves
2. the way a thing is done

mannered

mantelpiece   a shelf over the fireplace

manufacture   to make things in a factory

many   a lot: a big number

maple   a tree with broad leaves

marble
1. a hard stone which is usually beautifully marked
2. a small ball made of glass or clay, used for playing the game of 'marbles'

march   to walk like a soldier

marched
marches
marching

March   the third month of the year

mare   a female horse

margarine   a food that can be used instead of butter

margin   a blank space at the sides of a page

marigold   an orange-coloured flower

mark
1. a sign or a stain
2. to put a mark on something
3. to correct someone's work

marked
marker
marking

market	a place, often in the open, for buying and selling things	
marmalade	jam made with oranges	
maroon	1. a dark red colour 2. to leave someone alone on a desert island	**marooned** **marooning**
marriage	when two people get married	
marrow	a long-shaped green vegetable	
marry	to take a husband or wife	**married** **marries** **marrying**
marsh	a piece of boggy ground	**marshes** **marshy**
marvellous	wonderful	**marvellously**
mash	to press into small pieces and mix up	**mashed** **mashes** **mashing**
mask	a cover worn over the face so that the person cannot be recognised	**masked**
mass	1. a large amount of something 2. weight 3. a church service	**masses** **massive**
mast	a tall pole for the sails of a ship or for a flag	
master	a man in charge	
match	1. a piece of wood with a special tip which lights if it is rubbed 2. a game between two sides 3. to be alike in colour or shape	**matches** **matched** **matches** **matching**
mate	1. a partner 2. a friend 3. the person next in command to the captain of a ship	
material	the stuff of which a thing is made	

mathematics	the study of numbers and measurement	**mathe-matical**
matter	to be important	
mattress	the soft part of the bed on which you lie	**mattresses**
mauve	a light purple colour	
maximum	the greatest amount	
May	the fifth month of the year	
mayor	the chief person in a town	**mayoress**
maypole	a pole, with ribbons, for dancing round	
meadow	grassland	
meal	the food you eat at one time	
mean	1. selfish 2. to intend to do something	**meaning** **meant**
measles	an illness which shows by red spots on your body	
measure	to find out the size of something	**measured** **measure-ment** **measuring**
meat	the animal flesh we eat	
mechanic	someone who works with machines	**mechanical**
medal	a small piece of decorated metal given to brave people or to the winners of a game or sport	
meddle	to interfere with something that should be left alone	**meddled** **meddling**
medicine	a liquid or pill which you swallow when you are ill	
meet	1. to come together 2. to touch or join	**meeting** **met**
melon	a very large fruit	
melt	to make solid things into liquid by heating	**melted** **melting**
member	someone who belongs to a group	

memory	1. the power of remembering	**memories**
	2. something you can remember	**memorise**
mend	to repair	**mended**
		mender
		mending
mental	of the mind: worked out in your head and not on paper	
menu	a list of what there is to eat	
mercy	pity: forgiveness	**merciful**
mermaid	a sea-woman found in stories, with the tail of a fish	
merry	happy: full of fun	**merrier**
		merriest
		merrily
mess	a dirty or untidy muddle	**messy**
message	news sent from one person to another	
messenger	someone who carries a message	
metal	a material such as iron or steel or gold	
meteor	a shooting star	**meteorite**
meter	a machine for measuring	
method	a way of doing something	**methodical**
metre	measure of length in the metric system	**metric**
mice	more than one mouse	
microbe	a minute germ	
microphone	the instrument into which you speak when broadcasting	
microscope	an instrument for making tiny objects appear much larger	
midday	noon	
middle	the centre	
midnight	12 o'clock at night	
midsummer	half-way through the summer	

mi

might	1. great power or strength 2. (I *might* go for a walk if the weather were fine)	**mighty**
mile	a measure of distance	**mileage** **milestone**
milk	1. white liquid which we get mostly from cows 2. to get milk from an animal	**milked** **milking** **milkman**
mill	1. a place where corn is ground 2. a factory	**miller**
millilitre	measure of capacity in the metric system	
millimetre	measure of length in the metric system	
million	1 000 000	
millionaire	a person who is very rich	
mince	to cut into very small pieces	**minced** **mincer** **mincing**
mincemeat	a mixture of chopped dried fruits used in mince pies	
mind	1. the part of the brain with which you think 2. to be careful 3. to keep safe	**minded** **minder** **minding**
mine	1. a deep hole or tunnel in the ground from which coal and other minerals are dug 2. a sort of bomb placed under the ground or under water 3. belonging to me	**mined** **miner** **mining**
mineral	a material, such as coal or metal, that is dug from the ground	
mint	1. a plant used for making some foods tasty 2. the place where coins are made	

minus	take away (ten *minus* four leaves six)	
minute	1. 60 seconds 2. very small	
miracle	a wonderful happening that cannot be explained	**miraculous**
mirror	a looking glass	
misbehave	to behave badly	**misbehaved** **misbehaving** **misbehaviour**
mischief	something which causes people annoyance or harm	**mischievous**
miser	a very mean person who tries not to spend his money	**miserly**
miserable	unhappy	**miserably** **misery**
misfortune	bad luck	
miss	1. the title sometimes given to a girl or lady who is not married 2. to feel the loss of 3. not to hit	**misses** **missed** **misses** **missing**
mist	cloud at ground level	**misty**
mistake	1. something that has been done wrongly 2. to believe wrongly	**mistaken** **mistaking** **mistook**
mistletoe	a plant with white berries which we hang up at Christmas time	
mistress	1. a woman who teaches 2. a woman who looks after a house	**mistresses**
mitten	a glove which does not cover the ends of the fingers	
mix	to stir together	**mixed** **mixer** **mixes** **mixing** **mixture**

moan	1. a long, low sound made when you are very sad or in pain 2. to make such a sound	**moaned** **moaning**
moat	a large ditch round a castle	
mock	to make fun of	**mocked** **mocking**
model	1. a small copy of something 2. a good example 3. to shape	**modelled** **modelling**
modern	up-to-date	
moist	slightly wet	**moisten** **moisture**
mole	a small animal, with a pointed nose, that lives underground	
molten	melted	
moment	a very small space of time	
monastery	a building where monks live	**monasteries**
Monday	the second day of the week	
money	coins or banknotes	
mongrel	a dog of no special kind	
monitor	someone who does jobs for a teacher	
monk	a holy man who usually lives in a monastery	
monkey	a little animal that lives in trees in hot countries	
monster	a large, frightening creature	**monstrous**
month	one of the twelve parts of a year	**monthly**
moon	a planet that moves round the earth	**moonbeam** **moonlight** **moonlit**
moor	1. open heathland 2. to tie up a boat or ship	**moored** **mooring**
moose	a large deer	**moose**
mop	1. a bundle of cloth on the end of a stick for cleaning floors 2. to wipe with a mop	**mopped** **mopping**

more	greater than	
morning	before midday	
mosquito	a tiny insect that flies and bites	**mosquitoes**
moss	a short thick-growing plant found in shady or damp places	**mossy**
most	greatest or largest	**mostly**
moth	an insect like a butterfly which usually flies by night	
mother	a woman who has children	
motor	a machine that makes something move	**motor-boat** **motor-car** **motor-cycle** **motorist** **motorway**
mould	1. a hairy growth caused by damp 2. a shape in which things are pressed or put to set 3. to shape something by using a mould	**moulded** **moulding** **mouldy**
mount	1. to get on to a horse 2. to climb	**mounted** **mounting**
mountain	a high hill	**mountainous**
mouse	a small rat-like animal	**mice**
moustache	the hair on a man's top lip	
mouth	1. the opening through which we eat and speak 2. where a river meets the sea 3. the entrance to anything	
move	1. to put in another place 2. to go to live in another place	**movable** **moved** **movement** **moving**
mow	to cut grass with a machine	**mowed** **mower** **mowing** **mown**
much	a great deal	
muddle	1. untidiness: a jumble 2. to make a muddle	**muddled** **muddling**

muddy	thick with mud	**muddier** **muddiest**
multiply	to add together an amount a number of times	**multiplication** **multiplied** **multiplies** **multiplying**
mumble	to speak without opening your mouth properly	**mumbled** **mumbling**
mummy	1. a child's word for mother 2. a dead body which has been saved from decay	**mummies**
mumps	an illness which causes swellings of the face and neck	
murder	to kill someone	**murdered** **murderer** **murdering** **murderous**
muscle	(The boxer showed us the strong *muscle* in his arm)	
museum	a building where interesting things are put on show	
mushroom	a white and brown plant shaped like a tiny umbrella	
music	a pleasing sound played or sung	**musical**
musician	someone who plays music	
must	(You *must* do what you are told)	
mustard	a plant whose seed is used to make the hot yellow mixture sometimes eaten with meat	
mutton	meat we get from sheep	
myself	(I am sitting by *myself* as my partner is away)	
mystery	something that cannot be explained	**mysteries** **mysterious** **mysteriously**

n

nag	1. a horse	**nagged**
	2. to be always finding fault with	**nagging**
nail	1. a piece of metal driven into wood to hold it in place	**nailed**
		nailing
	2. the horny part at the end of the fingers and toes	
naked	bare	
name	1. a word by which someone or something is known	**named**
		naming
	2. to call something or someone by a name	
narrow	not wide	**narrower**
		narrowest
		narrowly
nasty	not pleasant	**nastier**
		nastiest
		nastily
nation	a country and its people	**national**
native	a native of a country is a person who was born in that country	
natural	1. not artificial	**naturally**
	2. at ease	
nature	everything in the world not made by people	
naughty	badly behaved	**naughtier**
		naughtiest
		naughtily
navigate	to guide the course of a ship or aircraft	**navigated**
		navigating
		navigation
navy	warships and their crews	**navies**
near	not far off	**nearby**
		nearer
		nearest
		nearly

neat	tidy: trim	**neater** **neatest** **neatly** **neatness**
necessary	cannot be done without	**necessity**
neck	the part of the body which joins the head and shoulders	
necklace	a thread of beads or jewels worn round the neck	
need	1. a want 2. to want	**needed** **needing** **needy**
needle	1. used for sewing with cotton or wool 2. a pointer on a dial	**needlework**
neglect	not to bother about	**neglected** **neglecting**
neigh	1. the sound a horse makes 2. to make a sound like a horse	**neighed** **neighing**
neighbour	a person who lives next door or nearby	**neighbour-** **hood**
neither	not one or the other	
nephew	the son of a brother or sister	
nerve	1. one of the parts of the body which carries messages to and from the brain 2. bravery: cheek	
nervous	easily frightened	**nervously**
nest	a home which birds make	**nested** **nesting**
netball	a ball game	
nettle	a stinging weed	
never	at no time	
new	fresh	**newer** **newest** **newly**
newsagent	a person who sells newspapers in a shop	

newspaper	a paper that gives news	
newsreel	a news film	
newt	a creature like a small lizard which lives in and out of water	
next	1. the one after 2. closest to	
nibble	to eat in small bites	**nibbled** **nibbling**
nice	pretty: pleasing	**nicely** **nicer** **nicest**
nickname	a name given in fun	
niece	the daughter of your brother or sister	
night	the time when it is dark	**nightdress** **nightgown** **nightly** **night-time**
nightingale	a bird with a lovely song	
nightmare	a frightening dream	
nine	9	**ninth**
nineteen	19	**nineteenth**
ninety	90	**ninetieth**
nobleman	a lord	**noblemen**
nobody	no one	
nod	to move your head up and down	**nodded** **nodding**
noise	a loud sound, usually unpleasant	**noisier** **noisiest** **noisily** **noisy**
none	not one	
nonsense	something silly	
noon	midday	
normal	usual	**normally**
north	opposite to south	
nose	part of the face with which you smell	
notch	a small 'v' shaped cut	**notches**

note
1. a short piece of writing
2. a musical sound
3. to look and remember

notebook
noted
notepaper
noting

nothing not anything at all

notice
1. a printed warning or guide
2. to see

noticed
noticing

nought nothing

November the eleventh month of the year

nowhere in no place

nozzle a spout at the end of a pipe

nucleus the centre around which things are grouped

nuclei
nuclear

nuisance someone or something that annoys you

numb not able to feel anything

numbed

number how many

numbered

numerator the number above the line in a fraction

nurse
1. one who looks after children or sick people
2. to look after someone who cannot look after herself
3. to hold a child in your arms

nursed
nursery
nursing

nylon a hard-wearing artificial thread

O

oak
1. a tree on which acorns grow
2. wood from the oak tree

oar a wooden pole with a wide flat end, used for rowing a boat

oasis a place in the desert where there is water, and things grow

oases

oath	1. a promise 2. a curse	
oats	a kind of corn used for food	
obedient	doing as you are told	obedience obediently
obey	to do as you are told	obeyed obeying
object	1. any article 2. an aim 3. to announce that you dislike something or someone	objected objecting objection
oblige	to do someone a favour	obliged obliging
oblong	a four-sided figure which is longer than it is broad	
oboe	a musical wind instrument	
obstacle	something that is in the way	
obstinate	stubborn	
obtain	to get	obtained obtaining
obvious	easy to see or understand	obviously
occupy	1. to live in 2. to take possession of a country	occupation occupied occupies occupying
ocean	a large sea	
o'clock	of the clock	
October	the tenth month of the year	
octopus	a sea animal with eight arms	octopuses
odd	1. queer 2. uneven 3. not one of a pair	oddly
off	1. not on 2. away	
offend	1. to hurt the feelings of 2. to do wrong	offended offending
offer	to say or show that you are ready to give or do anything that is needed	offered offering

office	a place where business is carried on
officer	a person in charge
often	many times
oil	1. a greasy liquid which keeps machinery running smoothly **oiled** **oiling** 2. to put oil on something **oily**
ointment	a grease that you put on a cut
old	having lasted for a long time **olden** **older** **oldest** **old-fashioned**
once	at one time only
one	a single thing: 1
onion	a white bulb with a strong smell, used as a vegetable
only	by itself
open	not shut or covered **opened** **opener** **opening** **openly**
operate	1. to work **operated** 2. to cut open the body of a sick person **operating** **operation** **operator**
opinion	what you think is true
opponent	a person who is against you
opposite	1. something that is quite different from something else 2. face to face with
orange	1. a fruit 2. the colour of an orange
orangeade	a drink made from orange juice
orbit	the path in which one thing moves round another in space
orchard	a field full of fruit trees

orchestra	a group of people playing musical instruments	
order	1. a command	**ordered**
	2. a tidy arrangement	**ordering**
	3. a list of things you want from a shop	
	4. to tell someone to do some-thing	
ordinary	usual: not surprising	
organ	a musical instrument worked by air and often used in churches	**organist**
ornament	1. a decoration which makes something more beautiful	
	2. a vase or piece of pottery in a room	
orphan	a child whose father and mother are dead	**orphanage**
		orphaned
ostrich	a very large bird which cannot fly	ostriches
other	1. different	**otherwise**
	2. more	
otter	an animal which lives in water	
ought	(You *ought* to help your parents when they are busy)	
ounce	a measure of mass (weight): 16 ounces make 1 pound	
our	belonging to us	
ourselves	us or we	
out	1. not in	**outdoors**
	2. not burning	**outer**
outing	a pleasure trip	
outlaw	a bandit: a person who does not keep the law	
outside	1. the outer part: the covering	
	2. not indoors	
oval	egg-shaped	
oven	a closed space in which we cook food	

over	1. above 2. across 3. finished
overalls	clothes to put on over your suit or dress to keep it clean
overboard	over the side of a ship
overcoat	a top coat
overhead	above your head: up in the sky
overseas	in a land across the sea
overtake	to catch up with and pass **overtaken** **overtaking** **overtook**
overtime	extra time spent by a person at a job
overturn	to turn upside-down **overturned** **overturning**
owe	not to have paid for some- **owed** thing which you have had **owing**
owl	a bird of prey which hoots and flies at night
own	1. to have something which **owned** belongs to you **owner** 2. to admit **owning** 3. (I like to have my *own* way)
ox	an animal like a cow **oxen**
oxygen	one of the gases in the air
oyster	a shell-fish

p

pace	a stride or step
pack	1. a set of playing cards **packed** 2. a bundle, usually carried on **packet** on the back **packing** 3. to put into boxes, bags or **unpack** cases

pad	1. a cover to protect your leg while playing cricket 2. to stuff with soft material	**padded** **padding**
paddle	1. a short oar 2. to use a paddle 3. to walk in shallow water with bare feet	**paddled** **paddling**
page	1. one side of a leaf in a book 2. a boy attendant	
paid	(John *paid* for his school dinners and then lost the change)	
pail	a bucket	
pain	suffering: an ache	**pained** **painful** **painfully** **paining** **painless**
paint	1. a liquid for colouring things 2. to put paint on to something	**paintbox** **painted** **painter** **painting**
pair	a set of two; two things that are alike or go together	
palace	a special house for a king or queen or bishop	
pale	faint in colour	**paleness**
palm	1. a tree that grows in hot countries 2. part of your hand	
pancake	a thin flat batter cake	
pane	a sheet of glass in a window	
panic	sudden fear and alarm	
pansy	a flower like a large violet	**pansies**
pant	to gasp in quick breaths	**panted** **panting**
panther	a kind of leopard	
pantomime	a play based on a fairy story, usually performed at Christmas time	

pantry	a room or large cupboard for storing food	pantries
paper	the stuff on which we write, draw or paint	
papyrus	an ancient kind of paper	
parachute	nylon cloth which opens in the shape of an umbrella to save a person who has to jump from an aircraft	**parachutist** **paratroops**
paragraph	a short part of a piece of writing	
paraffin	a thin oil used in heaters	
parallel	the same distance apart all along	**parallelo-gram**
parcel	something wrapped up in paper and tied with string	
pardon	1. forgiveness 2. to forgive or excuse some-one	**pardoned** **pardoning**
parent	a father or mother	
park	1. a piece of ground where people go to enjoy them-selves 2. to put a car in a place and leave it there	**car-park** **parked** **parking**
parliament	the people chosen by election who decide a country's laws	
parrot	a bird with bright feathers, often kept as a pet	
parsley	a plant used for flavouring food	
parsnip	a plant whose thick root is used as food	
part	1. a piece of something: a share 2. to separate	**parted** **parting** **partition** **partly**
particle	a very small piece	

partner	someone who shares work or play with another person	
party	a number of people having a jolly time together	parties
pass	1. a narrow path through the mountains 2. a ticket 3. to go by 4. to hand on 5. to get through an examination	passes **passed** **passes** **passing** **passport**
passage	1. a corridor 2. a voyage from one port to another	
passenger	a traveller on a train, bus, car, ship or aircraft	
past	(We start school at half *past* one)	
paste	1. sticky stuff which is put on to things to fix them together 2. to stick with paste	**pasted** **pasting**
pastry	1. the crust of pies or tarts 2. a pie, tart or cake	pastries
pasture	a field in which cattle feed	
patch	1. a piece of material sewn over a hole to mend it 2. to put a patch on something	patches **patched** **patches** **patching** **patchy**
path	a place for walking: a track	**pathway**
patience	1. calmness when you are annoyed, or in trouble, or waiting 2. a card game	**patiently**
patient	1. a person having treatment from a doctor 2. having patience	
pattern	1. something to be copied 2. a design	

pavement	a footpath of flat stones beside a road
paw	an animal's foot with claws
pay	to give money for something — **paid** **paying** **payment**
pea	a green seed which grows in a pod and which is eaten as a vegetable
peace	1. quietness and calm — **peaceful** 2. a time when there is no war — **peacefully**
peach	a fruit with a skin like velvet — **peaches**
peacock	a bird with a large tail which can open like a fan
peak	1. the top of a mountain — **peaked** 2. the front of a cap
peal	the sound of bells or thunder
pear	a juicy fruit with yellow or green skin
pearl	a whitish jewel which is found **pearly** inside the shell of a pearl oyster
pebble	a small round stone — **pebbly**
peck	to bite or pick up food with a **pecked** beak **pecking**
peculiar	odd: unusual
pedal	1. part of a machine, worked **pedalled** by the foot **pedalling** 2. to use a pedal
pedestrian	a person who is walking
peel	1. the outer skin of a fruit or **peeled** vegetable **peeler** 2. to take off the outer skin of **peeling** something
peep	to look at something quickly **peeped** while you are hidden **peeping**
pelt	1. the skin and fur of an animal **pelted** 2. to throw things at some- **pelting** body or something

penalty	punishment for breaking the law: a free kick at goal given against a team that has broken a rule	**penalties**
pence	pennies	
pencil	1. a pointed writing tool with a black or coloured centre 2. to use a pencil	**pencil-box** **pencilled** **pencilling**
pendulum	a hanging mass (weight) that swings freely	
penknife	a small pocket knife	**penknives**
penny	a coin: one hundred make one pound	**pennies**
penguin	a sea bird of the southern part of the world that can swim but not fly	
people	human beings	
pepper	(We put *pepper* and salt on our dinner)	
perch	1. anything on which a bird stands 2. to settle on a perch	**perches** **perched** **perches** **perching**
percussion	musical instruments which are struck to be played	
perfect	exactly right	**perfectly**
perform	1. to do something 2. to sing, act or dance in public	**perform-** **ance** **performed** **performer** **performing**
perfume	scent	
perhaps	possibly	
perimeter	the distance round the edge of something	
permission	(The teacher gave Tina *per-mission* to leave the room)	
permit	to allow	**permitted** **permitting**
perpendicular	exactly upright	

person	a human being	
perspire	to sweat	**perspiration** **perspired** **perspiring**
persuade	to talk to someone to get them to do what you want	**persuaded** **persuading**
pest	a person or thing which is a nuisance	
petal	a part of a flower	
petrol	the fuel used by motor cars	
'phone	the telephone	
photograph	a picture taken by a camera	**photo- grapher** **photo- graphy**
pianist	someone who plays a piano	
piano	a musical instrument played by pressing down keys	
pick	1. a pointed hammer for breaking hard ground 2. to choose 3. to gather fruit, flowers or vegetables	**picked** **picking**
pickle	vegetables kept in vinegar	
picnic	1. a meal eaten out in the country 2. to have a picnic	**picnicked** **picnicker** **picnicking**
picture	a drawing, painting or photo- graph	
piece	part of something	
pier	a long platform built out into the sea	
pigeon	a bird of the dove family	
pigmy	one of a race of very small people living in parts of Africa and Asia	**pigmies**
pigtail	a plait of hair	
pile	1. a heap 2. to make a heap	**piled** **piling**

pilgrim	a person who makes a journey to a holy place	**pilgrimage**
pill	medicine taken as a tablet	
pillar	a tall post made of stone to support part of a large building	
pillow	a cushion on which to rest your head in bed	**pillowcase**
pilot	a person who steers a plane or boat	
pimple	a sore little swelling on the skin	
pinafore	an apron or overall	
pincers	a tool for pulling out nails	
pinch	to squeeze sharply	**pinched** **pinches** **pinching**
pine	a tree on which cones grow and which has leaves like needles	
pineapple	a large fruit shaped like a pine cone	
pink	pale red	
pint	eight of them make a gallon	
pioneer	someone who does or tries something first	
pipe	1. a tube 2. something in which to smoke tobacco	**piping**
pirate	a sea-robber who steals from ships at sea	
pistol	a small gun	
piston	part of an engine which moves up and down in a cylinder	
pitch	1. a piece of ground on which a game is played 2. black tarry stuff used in making roads 3. to throw	**pitches** **pitched** **pitches** **pitching**

pity	a feeling of sorrow for a person who has had trouble or bad luck	
place	1. a spot or position 2. to put something in position	**placed** **placing**
plaice	a flat fish which is good to eat	**plaice**
plain	1. a stretch of level country 2. not pretty 3. easy to see or understand 4. simple	**plainly**
plait	a rope of hair made by twisting three lengths of it together	**plaited**
plan	1. a drawing to show how a thing looks from above 2. something you intend to do 3. to arrange to do something	**planned** **planner** **planning**
'plane	an aeroplane	
plane	1. a tool for smoothing wood 2. a tree like a sycamore 3. to smooth wood with a plane	**planed** **planing**
planet	a large object in space which, like the earth, moves round the sun	
plank	a long flat piece of wood	
plant	1. something that grows in the ground 2. to put something in the ground so that it will grow	**planted** **planting**
plaster	1. a strip of cloth with a sticky side for covering cuts 2. a coating for walls and ceilings	
plastic	a type of artificial material used for making toys, buckets, bowls and many other things	
plasticine	a material used for modelling	
plate	a flat dish on which food is put	**plateful**

platform	1. the raised part of a station on to which you step when getting off a train 2. the raised part of a floor, usually at one end of a hall	
play	1. a story told by acting 2. to join in a game	**played** **player** **playful** **playground** **playing** **playtime**
pleasant	cheerful: enjoyable	**pleasantly**
please	to give pleasure to someone	**pleased** **pleasing**
pleasure	enjoyment	
plenty	all that is needed and more	**plentiful**
pliers	a tool used for gripping things	
plimsoll	a light canvas shoe	
plod	to walk slowly and heavily	**plodded** **plodding**
plot	1. a small piece of land 2. a secret plan to do something 3. to make a plot	**plotted** **plotting**
plough	1. a machine used by farmers to turn over the soil 2. to use a plough	**ploughed** **ploughing**
pluck	1. courage 2. to pull out feathers 3. to pull a string or wire sharply	**plucked** **pluckily** **plucking** **plucky**
plug	1. something used to stop or fill up a hole 2. to put a plug in	**plugged** **plugging**
plum	a fruit with a stone in	
plumber	a person who fits and mends pipes for gas and water	
plump	fat: stout	
plunge	to move downwards very quickly	**plunged** **plunging**

plywood	strong board made by gluing layers of wood together	
poach	1. to steal animals or birds or fish from someone's land	**poached** **poacher**
	2. to cook opened eggs or fish in boiling water	**poaches** **poaching**
pocket	a little bag sewn into clothes	
poem	writing in verses where the lines usually rhyme with each other	
poet	a person who writes poems	
poetry	poems	
point	1. the sharp end of something	**pointed**
	2. part of the score in a game	**pointer**
	3. to show something with the finger	**pointing**
poison	1. something which, if eaten or drunk, will harm a living thing	**poisoned** **poisonous**
	2. to injure or kill a living thing with poison	
poke	to push the end of something into something else	**poked** **poking**
poker	a rod for poking a fire	
polar	to do with the North or South Pole	
pole	1. the parts of the earth which are furthest from the equator	
	2. a long round piece of wood	
police	people who help to keep law and order	**police**
polish	1. something used to make things shine	**polished** **polishes**
	2. to rub something to make it shine	**polishing**
polite	well-mannered	**politely** **politeness**
polythene	a strong plastic material	
pond	a small lake	
pony	a small horse	**ponies**

pool	a pond	
poor	1. having only a little money	**poorer**
	2. not well done	**poorest**
	3. not good	**poorly**
pop	short for popular	
poplar	a tall tree	
poppy	a plant with bright red flowers	**poppies**
popular	well-liked	
population	the number of people living in a place	
porch	the covered entrance to a building	**porches**
porcupine	an animal like a large hedge-hog	
pork	meat from a pig	
porpoise	a sea animal like a small whale	
porridge	cooked oats usually eaten for breakfast	
port	1. a town with a harbour or docks	
	2. the left-hand side of a ship or aeroplane	
	3. a wine	
portable	easy to carry	
porter	a person who carries luggage	
position	a place: a spot	
possess	to own something	**possessed**
		possesses
		possessing
		possession
		possessive
possible	1. able to be done	**impossible**
	2. able to happen	**possibility**
		possibly
post	1. a strong pole	**postbox**
	2. the carrying of letters and parcels	**postcard**
		posted
	3. the day's letters	**posting**
	4. to send letters or parcels by post	**postman**

poster	a large notice to advertise something	
potato	a vegetable which grows under the ground	**potatoes**
pottery	clay shaped into such things as cups, vases and plates and baked hard	
pouch	a small bag	**pouches**
pounce	to spring forward suddenly	**pounced** **pouncing**
pound	1. a measure of weight: 16 ounces 2. 100 pennies	
pour	1. to tip a liquid out of its container 2. to rain heavily	**poured** **pouring**
powder	1. dust made by crushing something 2. to crush something to powder	**powdered** **powdering** **powdery**
power	strength	**powerful** **powerless**
practically	almost	
practice	doing something many times	
practise	to do something many times in order to become better at it	**practised** **practising**
prairie	a wide area of flat grassland	
praise	to say something is good or well done	**praised** **praising**
pram	used for wheeling babies about	
pray	to speak to God, silently or aloud	**prayed** **prayer** **praying**
preach	to give a sermon	**preached** **preacher** **preaches** **preaching**
precious	valuable	
precipice	a steep cliff	

prefect	a pupil who makes other school-children keep the school rules	
prefer	to like one thing or person better than another	**preferred** **preferring**
prepare	to get ready	**preparation** **prepared** **preparing**
present	1. a gift 2. now 3. here: not away 4. to give something	**presented** **presenting** **presently**
press	1. a machine for pressing, such as a printing machine 2. to squeeze or push something 3. to flatten or smooth with an iron	**presses** **pressed** **presses** **pressing**
pretend	to make-believe	**pretended** **pretending**
pretty	pleasing to look at	**prettier** **prettiest** **prettily** **prettiness**
prevent	to stop something from happening	**prevented** **preventing** **prevention**
prey	an animal that is being hunted	
price	the cost of something	**priceless**
prick	to make a small hole with a sharp point	**pricked** **pricking**
prickle	a thorn	**prickly**
pride	a feeling that you have done something well	
priest	1. a Protestant or a Roman Catholic clergyman 2. a man appointed to organise worship in many religions	**priestess**
prime	a prime number is one that has no factors except itself and 1	

primrose	a pale yellow spring flower	
prince	a boy of royal birth	
princess	a royal female	**princesses**
print	to make words or pictures with a printing machine	**printed** **printer** **printing**
prison	a place where criminals are kept	**prisoner**
private	not for everybody to know or use	**privately**
prize	a reward to be won	
probable	likely to happen	**probably**
problem	a puzzle: a question which needs to be carefully thought about	
proceed	to go on: to go forward	
procession	a group of people or things moving forward	
prod	to poke with something pointed like a stick	**prodded** **prodding**
produce	1. food that is grown 2. to make or show	**produced** **producing** **product** **production**
professor	an important teacher in a college or university	
profit	1. gain 2. to gain	**profited** **profiting**
programme	1. a plan 2. a list of items in a concert or play	
progress	1. improvement 2. to move forward: to get better	**progressed** **progresses** **progressing**
project	a plan of something to be done	
projector	a machine for showing films on a screen	
promenade	a paved road for walking on by the sea	

promise	to mean it when you say that you will do something	**promised** **promising**
prong	one of the points of a fork	**pronged**
proof	something that shows a thing is true	
propeller	blades which go round to move along an aircraft or ship	
proper	right: correct: suitable	**properly**
property	something owned by someone	**properties**
prosecute	to say in court that someone has done something against the law	**prosecuted** **prosecuting** **prosecution**
protect	to keep someone or something from harm or damage	**protected** **protecting** **protection**
protest	to object to something	**protested** **protesting**
proud	thinking highly of yourself	**proudly**
prove	to show that something is true	**proved** **proving**
proverb	a well-known saying which teaches a lesson	
provide	to supply	**provided** **providing**
prow	the front part of a boat	
prowl	to creep about, usually in search of something	**prowled** **prowler** **prowling**
prune	a dried plum	
public	1. all the people 2. for everyone to use	
pudding	a soft sweet food	
puddle	a little pool of water	
puff	1. a quick short blow of air or smoke 2. a soft pad for putting on face powder 3. to blow out steam or smoke in puffs	**puffed** **puffing**

pull	to tug towards yourself	**pulled** **pulling**
pulley	a wheel with a rope round it for lifting things	
pullover	a jersey or sweater	
pulse	the throbbing of blood through the body	
pump	1. a machine for forcing air or water through a tube 2. an indoor or dancing shoe 3. to use a pump	**pumped** **pumping**
punch	1. a blow with the fist 2. to use the fist for hitting	**punches** **punched** **punches** **punching**
punctual	on time	**punctuality**
puncture	1. a small hole made with a sharp point 2. to make a hole	**punctured** **puncturing**
punish	to make someone suffer for what he has done wrong	**punished** **punishes** **punishing** **punishment**
pupil	1. a person who is being taught 2. part of the eye	
puppet	a doll made to move, usually by strings	
puppy	a young dog	**puppies**
purchase	to buy	**purchased** **purchasing**
pure	clean: not mixed with anything else	
purple	the colour made when red and blue are mixed	
purpose	something that you mean to do	**purposely**
purr	1. the sound a cat makes when it is happy 2. to make a sound like a cat	**purred** **purring**

purse	a small bag for carrying money	
push	to press against something	**pushed** **pushes** **pushing**
put	to place in position	**putting**
putty	paste used for fixing glass in frames	
puzzle	1. a problem: something that is hard to work out 2. to think hard about a difficult question	**puzzled** **puzzling**
pyjamas	a suit to sleep in	
pylon	a tall tower, usually for carrying electric cables	
pyramid	a solid shape with triangular sides which meet at a point	
python	a large snake	

q

quack	1. the noise made by a duck 2. to make a noise like a duck	**quacked** **quacking**
quaint	odd: unusual: old-fashioned	
quantity	amount	**quantities**
quarrel	1. an angry disagreement 2. to argue: to disagree	**quarrelled** **quarrelling** **quarrelsome**
quarry	a place where stone is cut from the ground	**quarries**
quart	two pints	
quarter	one of four equal parts of anything	
quay	a place where ships load and unload	**quayside**
queen	1. the head woman of a country 2. the wife of a king	
queer	odd	**queerly**

quench	1. to cure a thirst 2. to put out a fire	**quenched** **quenches** **quenching**
question	1. something you say that needs an answer 2. to ask a question	**questioned** **questioning**
queue	1. a line of people waiting their turn 2. to form part of a queue	**queued** **queueing**
quick	speedy: lively	**quicker** **quickest** **quickly** **quickness**
quiet	1. making little or no noise 2. still	**quieter** **quietest** **quietly**
quill	a large feather	
quilt	a padded bed cover	**quilted**
quite	completely	
quiz	questions that test someone's knowledge	**quizzes**

r

rabbit	a small, furry, long-eared animal that lives in a burrow	
race	1. a kind of people 2. a test to see who is the fastest	**raced** **racer** **racing**
rack	a frame with bars or pegs for holding things	
racket	1. a lot of noise 2. a stringed bat used in games like tennis (some- times spelt racquet)	
radar	a way of finding the position of aircraft or ships by elec- trical echoes	

radiator	1. a number of hot-water pipes joined together and used for heating a room 2. the place in a motor-car, usually in the front, where hot water from the engine is cooled	
radio	a wireless set	
radish	a small vegetable eaten raw	radishes
radius	the distance from the centre of a circle to its edge	radii
raffia	narrow strips from palm-leaves, used for weaving into mats and baskets	
raft	floating logs or boards fastened together	
rafter	a beam of a roof	
rage	1. temper: great anger 2. to shout in great anger	raged raging
ragged	in torn clothes	
raid	1. a sudden attack 2. to attack suddenly	raided raider raiding
rail	a bar of wood or metal to hold on to or for a train to run on	railing railway
rain	1. drops of water falling from the clouds 2. to pour or shower down from above	raincoat raindrop rained rainfall raining rainy
rainbow	a coloured arch formed in the sky when the sun shines on falling rain	
raise	1. to lift up 2. to collect 3. to bring up	raised raising
raisin	a dried grape	

rake
1. a garden tool with a metal comb at the end
2. to use a rake

raked
raking

ram
a male sheep

ramble
1. a stroll
2. to roam or wander about

rambled
rambler
rambling

ramp
a short slope

ranch
a large cattle farm

ranches

rang
(I *rang* the bell at playtime)

rank
a person's title or position

ransom
money paid to set someone free

rare
uncommon: valuable

rarely

rascal
a rogue

rash
1. a lot of red spots on the skin
2. thoughtless

rashly

rasher
a thin slice of bacon or ham

raspberry
a small, sweet red fruit

raspberries

rate
1. speed
2. a set price

rather
(I would *rather* drink milk than water)

rattle
1. a baby's toy
2. a sharp clattering sound
3. to make a clattering sound

rattled
rattling

raven
a large black bird

ravine
a deep gorge

raw
1. not cooked
2. very cold and damp

ray
a beam of light

razor
an instrument with a sharp blade used for shaving

reach
to get as far as

reached
reaches
reaching

reach for
to stretch out to touch something

read	to say to yourself, or out loud, what you see written	**reader** **reading**
ready	prepared: in a fit state	**readily**
real	not made up: true	**really**
realise	to understand clearly	**realised** **realising**
reap	to cut down and collect a crop	**reaped** **reaper** **reaping**
rear	1. at the back 2. to raise	**reared** **rearing**
reason	1. why something is done 2. common sense	**reasonable**
rebel	someone who fights those in charge	**rebellion**
receipt	a ticket to show that something has been received	
receive	to have something given to you	**received** **receiving**
recent	happening only a little while ago	**recently**
reception	a party held so that people may be received by someone	
recipe	instructions on how to make something to eat or drink	
recite	to say aloud from memory	**recited** **reciting**
reckon	to count up	**reckoned** **reckoning**
recognise	to know someone, or something, again by sight	**recognised** **recognising**
record	1. a round disc played on a record player 2. a note written about anything that has happened	**recording**
recorder	a musical instrument made of wood or plastic	
recover	1. to get something back safely 2. to get well again	**recovered** **recovering** **recovery**

recreation	a pleasant way of passing time	
rectangle	an oblong shape with all its angles square	**rectangular**
red	the colour of a tomato or poppy	
reduce	to make smaller	**reduced** **reducing** **reduction**
reed	a tall grass which grows near water	
reel	1. a round, wooden holder on which cotton is wound 2. a Scottish dance	
re-entry	coming back from space into the earth's atmosphere	
referee	someone who sees that the rules are followed in a game	**refereed** **refereeing**
reflect	to throw back rays of light or sound	**reflected** **reflecting** **reflection**
refreshment	something light to eat or drink	
refrigerator	a cold store cupboard for food	
refugee	someone who has to leave his country because of danger	
refuse	1. rubbish 2. to say 'No' when you are asked to do something	**refused** **refusing**
region	a district	
register	a list of names	
regular	at even intervals	**regularly**
rehearse	to practise something for a play or concert	**rehearsal** **rehearsed** **rehearsing**
reign	1. the length of time a king or queen rules 2. to rule	**reigned** **reigning**

reindeer	a deer used for drawing sledges in the cold countries of the north	reindeer
reins	the leather straps that guide a horse	
relation	one who is linked by birth or marriage	
relative	a relation	
relay	a team race in which members of a team each run part of the way	
release	to let go: to set free	released releasing
reliable	able to be trusted or relied upon	
religion	belief in god	
rely	to put your trust in someone or something	relied relies relying
remain	1. to stay behind 2. to be left over at the end	remainder remained remaining
remark	something that is said	
remarkable	unusual: worth mentioning	
remember	to use your memory	remembered remember- ing
remind	to jog someone's memory	reminded reminder reminding
remove	to take off or to take away	removal removed removing
rent	money you pay for living in someone else's house	rented renting
repair	to mend	repaired repairing
repay	to pay back	repaid repaying

repeat	to say, or do, again	**repeated** **repeater** **repeating**
replay	to play again	**replayed** **replaying**
reply	1. an answer 2. to answer	**replies** **replied** **replies** **replying**
report	1. a loud bang 2. the results of your work which are sent to your parents 3. to tell or write about an event	**reported** **reporter** **reporting**
reptile	an animal, such as a snake, whose blood is only as warm as its surroundings	
require	to need	**required** **requiring**
rescue	to save someone or something from danger	**rescued** **rescuer** **rescuing**
reservoir	a place where a large amount of water is stored	
resolution	something you decide that you will try your hardest to do	
respectable	worth admiring	
rest	1. what is left over 2. to lie still and quiet	**rested** **restful** **resting** **restless**
restaurant	a place where you can eat a meal	
result	1. the score at the end of a game 2. the answer to a sum 3. to end in	**resulted** **resulting**
return	to go, or come, back	**returned** **returning**
revenge	something you do to get your own back	

reverse	to go backwards	**reversed** **reversing**
revolver	a small gun which fires several shots without re-loading	
reward	1. a prize for something done well 2. to give someone a reward	**rewarded** **rewarding**
rheumatism	a lasting pain in your bones or muscles	
rhinoceros	a very large, thick-skinned animal with a horn on its nose	rhinoceroses
rhubarb	a garden plant, with thick, red juicy stalks which can be cooked and eaten	
rhyme	words which end with the same sound rhyme	
rhythm	a regular beat in music or poetry	
ribbon	a long narrow strip of material	
rice	the seeds of the rice plant, which are an important food in many countries	
rich	wealthy	**richer** **richest** **richly**
riddle	a puzzle	
ride	to sit on something and be carried along	**ridden** **rider** **riding** **rode**
ridge	the line where two slopes meet	
ridiculous	very silly	
rifle	a gun with a long barrel	
right	1. correct 2. the opposite side to the left	
rind	the outside skin	

ring	1. a circle	
	2. a circle of metal worn on the finger	
	3. the sound made by a bell	**rang**
	4. to make a bell sound	**ringing**
		rung
ringlet	a curl of hair	
rinse	to wash out soap or dirt with clean water	**rinsed**
		rinsing
rip	to tear something	**ripped**
		ripping
ripe	ready to be eaten	
rise	1. an increase, usually in wages or prices	**risen**
		rising
	2. to get up, or stand up	**rose**
	3. to go up in the air	
risk	1. a danger	**risked**
	2. to take a chance	**risking**
		risky
river	a large stream flowing towards the sea	
road	a hard track for cars and lorries	**roadside**
roam	to stroll or wander about	**roamed**
		roaming
roar	1. a loud deep noise, like the noise a lion makes	**roared**
		roaring
	2. to make a very loud noise	
roast	to cook anything at an open fire or in an oven	**roasted**
		roasting
rob	to steal by force	**robbed**
		robber
		robbing
robbery	stealing by force	**robberies**
robin	a little bird with a red breast	
robot	a machine that seems to act like a real person	
rock	1. stone	**rocked**
	2. to sway gently backwards and forwards	**rockery**
		rocking
		rocky

rocket	1. a firework which shoots up in the air 2. a tube-shaped machine which is driven along by a jet of gases and which travels over great distances
rode	(Turpin *rode* his horse to York)
rogue	a rascal: someone who cheats and is a bad person
roll	1. anything wrapped round to make a tube-shape **rolled roller** 2. a list of names, such as a school register **rolling** 3. to turn over and over
roof	the covering on top of a house
rook	a large black bird with a hoarse cry **rookery**
room	1. one of the parts of a building **roomy** 2. enough space to hold anything
root	the underground part of a plant **rooted**
rope	a thick, strong cord **roped**
rose	1. a plant with a prickly stem and sweet-smelling flowers **rosy** 2. (The kite *rose* high into the air)
rot	to go bad **rotted rotten rotting**
rotate	to turn like a wheel **rotated rotating rotation**
rough	1. not smooth or level **roughly** 2. rude: not gentle 3. stormy
round	1. a part of a boxing match 2. shaped like a ring or like a ball 3. on every side of something: around

roundabout   1. a fairground machine with wooden horses or cars going round in a circle
2. a circle of road to help traffic where several roads meet

route   a path or road from one place to another

row   1. a line of people or things
2. a loud quarrel
3. to move a boat through water by using oars   **rowed rowing**

royal   to do with a king or queen   **royalty**

rub   to press and slide two things against each other   **rubbed rubbing**

rubber   1. the sap of the rubber tree from which tyres, balls and football bladders are made
2. a soft piece of rubber to clean off pencil marks

rubbish   anything which has no use: litter

ruby   a red precious stone   **rubies**

rucksack   a bag carried on the back, usually by climbers or hikers

rudder   the upright, movable blade which steers an aeroplane or boat

rude   bad-mannered: rough   **rudely**

rugby football }
rugger }   a winter game played with an oval leather ball

ruin   1. a tumble-down building
2. to spoil or destroy someone or something   **ruined ruining**

rule   1. an order which you must obey: a law   **ruled ruling**
2. to govern like a king or queen
3. to draw a straight line using a ruler

ruler	1. a length of wood or metal for measuring and drawing straight lines 2. someone who rules over other people
rumour	news which spreads quickly without anyone being sure that it is true

run
1. scored by a batsman in a game of cricket
2. to move along quickly

ran
runner
running

rung
1. a step on a ladder
2. (The school bell is *rung* every morning)

runway the track on an airfield where aircraft land and take off

rush
1. a plant that grows in wet places, used for making mats and baskets
2. to dash forward at a great speed

rushes
rushed
rushes
rushing

rust
1. a reddish-brown coat that forms on some metals after they have been left wet
2. to become covered with rust

rusted
rusting
rusty

rye a grain used for food

S

sabotage to damage something on purpose

sabotaged
sabotaging
saboteur

sack a large, strong bag, made of coarse cloth or thick paper

sad unhappy: full of sorrow

sadder
saddest
sadly
sadness

saddle	a seat for the rider of a horse or bicycle

safe	1. free from harm **safely**
	2. a strong cupboard in which **safer**
	   money is kept safely **safest**
	                                          safety

said	(Mary *said* that she was going home at tea-time)

sail	1. a sheet of cloth on a ship's **sailed**
	   mast to catch the wind **sailing**
	2. to travel in a boat or by
	   ship

sailor	one of a ship's crew
saint	a very holy person
salad	a mixture of vegetables or fruit, which is eaten cold
sale	when things are sold cheaply
salmon	a fish with pink flesh **salmon**
salt	the mineral which gives sea- **salted** water its taste **salty**
salute	to put your right hand to your **saluted** forehead as a way of greeting **saluting**
same	exactly alike
sand	powdered rock found on **sandy** beaches and in deserts
sandal	a light open shoe with straps
sandwich	meat, or other food, between **sandwiches** two slices of bread
sang	(The boys *sang* the hymns well)
sank	(The boat *sank* to the bottom of the sea)
sardine	a small fish, usually sold in a tin
sash	a waist or shoulder band, **sashes** made of cloth or ribbon
satchel	a shoulder-bag, usually made of leather, for carrying books to school

satellite	1. a small planet which goes round and round a larger one 2. an artificial object which travels in outer space round the earth
satin	a kind of shining silk cloth
satisfy	to please somebody by doing what is necessary **satisfaction** **satisfactory** **satisfied** **satisfies** **satisfying**
Saturday	the last day of the week
sauce	a liquid served with food to make it tastier **saucy**
saucepan	a long-handled metal pot, used for cooking
saucer	a small, shallow plate for a cup to stand on
sausage	minced meat in a skin case
savage	1. a wild or fierce person **savagely** 2. wild: fierce
save	1. to rescue someone from danger **saved** **saving** 2. to keep something so that you can use it later on
saw	1. a metal blade with teeth for cutting **sawdust** **sawed** 2. to cut with a saw **sawing** 3. (Peter looked out of the **sawn** window and *saw* his brother fall over)
saxophone	a musical wind instrument
say	to speak **said** **saying**
scab	a dry crust which forms over a cut in the skin
scald	1. the mark on your skin **scalded** caused by burning yourself **scalding** with steam or very hot liquid 2. to burn yourself with steam or very hot liquid

scale	1. a weighing machine
	2. a set of notes in music
	3. one of the horny discs that protect the skin of fish and snakes
scalene	a triangle with none of its sides or angles equal
scar	the mark left after a burn, cut or scratch has healed · **scarred**
scarce	1. less than is needed · **scarcely**
	2. hard to find · **scarcity**
scare	to frighten · **scarecrow** **scared** **scaring**
scarf	a long strip of woollen material to wear round your neck for warmth · **scarves**
scarlet	bright red
scatter	1. to throw around · **scattered**
	2. to move quickly in all direc- · **scattering** tions
scene	1. a view · **scenery**
	2. the place where something has happened
	3. a part of a stage play
scent	a smell, usually pleasant · **scented**
scholar	someone who learns · **scholarship**
school	a place where children or students are taught
schooner	a kind of large sailing boat
science	things we know which have been found out by experiments · **scientific** **scientist**
scissors	two blades joined together, with handles to move them, for cutting
scold	to grumble at someone for what they have done · **scolded** **scolding**
scone	a small, soft sort of cake, often spread with butter

scooter   a flat board on two wheels with a handlebar, which is pushed along with one foot

scorch
1. a brown mark on something made by burning it slightly   **scorches** **scorched**
2. to mark by scorching   **scorches** **scorching**

score
1. the number of goals, runs or points made in a game   **scored** **scorer**
2. twenty: 20   **scoring**
3. to get goals, runs or points in games

scout
1. a soldier sent out to spy on the enemy   **scouted** **scouting**
2. someone in the Scouts   **scoutmaster**

scramble
1. to get over uneven ground using hands as well as feet   **scrambled** **scrambling**
2. to rush and push to be the first one to get something

scrap   a small piece: something left over

scrape   to smooth, clean or graze something with a sharp-edged tool   **scraped** **scraping**

scratch
1. a small mark made with something sharp or pointed   **scratches** **scratched**
2. to make a scratch   **scratches** **scratching**

scream
1. a loud, shrill cry   **screamed**
2. to give a loud, shrill cry   **screaming**

screech   to give a high-pitched scream   **screeched** **screeches** **screeching**

screen
1. a partition, which can be folded up and moved
2. where you see the picture on a television set or in a cinema

screw	1. a nail with ridges round it, used for fastening pieces of wood together securely 2. a ship's propeller 3. to turn or twist round	**screwdriver** **screwed** **screwing**
scribble	to write carelessly	**scribbled** **scribbling**
scripture(s)	the books of the Bible	
scrub	to rub something with a wet, soapy brush, to make it clean	**scrubbed** **scrubbing**
scullery	a place for washing dishes	**sculleries**
scuttle	a bucket for holding coal	
sea	the salt water that covers about three-quarters of the world	**seagull** **seashore** **seasick** **seaside** **seaweed**
seal	1. an animal which lives both in the sea and on land, and eats fish 2. to fasten something so that it cannot be opened without breaking the fastening	**sealed** **sealing**
seam	the line where two pieces of cloth are sewn together	
search	to hunt for something	**searched** **searches** **searching**
season	spring, summer, autumn or winter	
seat	something to sit on	
seaweed	plants which grow in the sea	
second	1. there are sixty in a minute 2. next after the first	
secret	something you do not want anyone else to know	**secretly**
secure	firmly fixed: safe	
see	1. to look at 2. to understand	**saw** **seeing** **seen**

seed	a tiny grain made by a plant which will grow into another plant of the same kind	
seek	to look for	**seeking** **sought**
seem	to appear to be	**seemed** **seeming**
seesaw	a balanced plank, with a seat at each end, which can be made to rock up and down	
seize	to grab quickly	**seized** **seizing**
seldom	not often	
selfish	thinking too much about yourself and what you want	**selfishly**
sell	to give something in exchange for money	**selling** **sold**
semi-	half	
send	to start someone or something on the way	**sending** **sent**
senior	an older person: older	
sense	1. (He lost his *sense* of smell when he had a cold) 2. (There is no *sense* in wasting time)	**senseless**
sensible	showing good sense: wise	
sent	(The girl was *sent* to see the headmaster)	
sentence	1. a set of words that make complete sense 2. a punishment given by a judge	
sentry	a person who keeps guard	**sentries**
separate	1. not joined to anything: apart 2. to part, or cut off anything	**separated** **separately** **separating**
September	the ninth month of the year	
septic	festered: gone bad because of germs and dirt	

sergeant
1. a soldier, with three stripes on the sleeve, in charge of other soldiers
2. a police officer

serial
a story seen or heard one part at a time

serious
1. important and needing attention: grave
2. quiet and thoughtful: not joking

seriously

sermon
a talk by a preacher, usually in church

serpent
another name for a snake

servant
someone who is paid to work in a house

serve
1. to sell things in a shop
2. to give out helpings of food at the table
3. to do work for someone

served
server
service
serving

serviette
a piece of cloth or paper to protect your clothes while you are eating

set
1. a group of things which are alike in some way
2. to become firm or hard
3. to sink below the horizon, as the sun does
4. to put things in their proper place

setting

settee
a long, comfortable seat with a back, for two or more people

settle
1. to stop moving about
2. to decide how you are going to deal with something

settled
settling

seven 7
seventh

seventeen 17
seventeenth

seventy 70
seventieth

several
three or four: a small number of

sew	to use a needle and thread	**sewed** **sewing** **sewn**
shabby	nearly worn out	
shade	1. a cover for a light 2. a place without sunlight	**shaded** **shading** **shady**
shadow	a patch of shade caused by anything with a light behind it	
shady	sheltered from the light: cool	
shake	1. to move anything very quickly up and down 2. to tremble	**shaken** **shaker** **shakily** **shaking** **shaky** **shook**
shall	(I *shall* come to school tomorrow)	
shallow	not deep	
shame	a feeling of sorrow when you have done something wrong	
shampoo	1. a liquid soap for washing hair 2. to wash your hair with a shampoo	**shampooed** **shampooing**
shamrock	a plant like clover, which grows mainly in Ireland	
shape	1. the form of something 2. to mould anything	**shaped** **shaping**
share	1. one of the parts into which a thing is divided 2. to divide anything into parts	**shared** **sharing**
shark	a large fish which has rows of sharp teeth	
sharp	1. not blunt: pointed 2. quick to understand or move 3. sour 4. above the note in music	**sharper** **sharpest** **sharply**
sharpen	to make anything sharp	**sharpened** **sharpener** **sharpening**

shatter	to break into small pieces	**shattered** **shattering**
shave	to cut off hair with a razor	**shaved** **shaver** **shaving**
shawl	a piece of cloth to wear round the shoulders	
sheaf	a bundle of papers or corn	**sheaves**
shears	clippers for cutting wool, hedges or grass	
shed	a shelter used for storing things, usually made of wood	
sheep	the animal which gives us mutton and wool	**sheep**
sheet	a large piece of cloth or paper	
shelf	a flat ledge in a cupboard or on the wall, for holding things	**shelves**
shell	a hard cover to protect something soft	**shelled** **shelling**
shelter	a place where you can hide from danger or bad weather	**sheltered** **sheltering**
shepherd	a person who looks after sheep	**shepherdess**
sheriff	the person whose job it was to keep the peace in a county or district	
shield	1. a piece of armour carried on the arm 2. anything used to protect someone from danger	
shift	1. the length of time people work 2. a number of people working together 3. to move something heavy	**shifted** **shifting**
shin	the front of your leg from your knee to your ankle	
shine	1. to glow with light 2. to polish	**shining** **shiny** **shone**
shingle	small stones on a beach	

ship	a large boat for sea voyages	**shipping** **shipwreck** **shipwrecked**
shirt	a piece of clothing of thin cloth	
shiver	1. trembling caused by cold or fear 2. to tremble	**shivered** **shivering**
shock	1. an unpleasant surprise 2. to give someone an unpleasant surprise	**shocked** **shocking**
shoe	a covering worn on the foot	
shone	(The sun *shone* brightly last Sunday)	
shook	(Father *shook* me to wake me)	
shoot	to fire a gun or let loose an arrow	**shooting** **shot**
shop	1. a place where things are sold 2. to go to the shops to buy things	**shopkeeper** **shopped** **shopping**
shore	the land at the edge of the sea or a lake	
short	1. not long in length 2. not lasting long 3. less than is needed: scarce	**shortage** **shorter** **shortest** **shortly**
shorts	very short trousers	
shot	(The farmer *shot* a rabbit with her gun)	**shotgun**
should	(I *should* like to go to the Zoo)	
shoulder	the place where your arm is joined to your body	
shout	1. a loud cry 2. to call out loudly	**shouted** **shouting**
shove	1. a push 2. to push something to move it	**shoved** **shoving**

shovel
1. a spade with curved-up edges **shovelled**
2. to move things using a shovel **shovelling**

show
1. an entertainment **showed**
2. to let something be seen **showing**
3. to make something clear by explaining it **shown**

shower
rain falling for only a short time **showery**

shrimp
a small grey shellfish which turns pink when it is cooked

shrink
to get smaller **shrank**
shrinking

shrub
a plant like a small tree, but with no trunk: a bush

shunt
to use an engine to push loose wagons and carriages to a different railway line **shunted**
shunter
shunting

shut
1. closed **shutting**
2. to close anything

sick
ill **sickly**
sickness

side
1. an edge or border **sideways**
2. a group of players in a game

sideboard
a cupboard for holding everything you need to lay a table

siding
railway lines off the main line where wagons can be parked

sigh
to take a very deep breath because you are tired or sad **sighed**
sighing

sight
1. something you see **sighted**
2. being able to see **sighting**
3. to get a view of something

sign
1. a mark which has a meaning
2. a thing or event which tells you something will happen
3. a movement you make to let someone know what you want
4. to write your name

signature
signed
signing

signal
1. a message sent by signs
2. to send a message by signs
3. a sign used on a railway

signalled
signalling
signalman

silent   not making any sound

silence
silently

silk   a smooth, soft cloth, made from the thin thread spun by the caterpillar of a silk moth

silkworm
silky

silly   foolish

sillier
silliest
silliness

silver
1. a shiny, precious metal
2. the colour of silver
3. all the coins which are silver-coloured

silvery

similar   the same, or nearly the same

simple
1. very easy to do or understand
2. silly: foolish

simply

since   (I have not been swimming *since* last summer)

sincere   honest: not pretending

sincerely

sing   to make a tune with your voice

sang
singer
singing
sung

single
1. one only
2. not married

sink
1. a bowl with a tap and drain in a kitchen
2. to fall downwards through water

sank
sinking
sunk

sip   to drink in small amounts

sipped
sipping

sister	(My *sister* and I are the only children my parents have)	
sit	to be seated	**sat** **sitting**
six	6	**sixth**
sixteen	16	**sixteenth**
sixty	60	**sixtieth**
size	the measurement of anything	
skate	1. a blade, or four wheels, fixed on a shoe, so that you can glide or roll along 2. to roll or glide on skates over the ground or on ice	**skated** **skater** **skating**
skeleton	the bones in a body	
skid	to slide suddenly on something smooth or slippery	**skidded** **skidding**
skill	cleverness at doing something	**skilful** **skilled**
skim	1. to take off anything floating on top of a liquid 2. to glide over something, hardly touching it	**skimmed** **skimming**
skin	1. the outer covering on the body of a person or animal 2. the outer covering of fruit 3. to take off skin or peel	**skinned** **skinning**
skin-diver	someone who dives and swims underwater without a diving suit	
skip	1. to jump lightly from one foot to the other 2. to use a skipping rope	**skipped** **skipping**
skipper	the captain of a boat or ship	
skirt	a piece of clothing which hangs from the waist	
skull	the bones of the head	
sky	the space round the earth, where the clouds float	**skies**

skylark	a small bird which soars very high into the air and sings as it flies
skyscraper	a very tall building
slack	1. loose: not tight **slacked** 2. lazy and careless about **slacker** work **slacking**
slacks	trousers worn by women
slam	to close something with great **slammed** force **slamming**
slant	1. a slope **slanted** 2. to put something with one **slanting** end higher than the other
slap	1. a blow given with an open **slapped** hand **slapping** 2. to smack someone with the flat of your hand
slave	1. a person who belongs to a **slaved** master and who must work **slavery** for him **slaving** 2. to work very hard
sledge	a low carriage with runners **sledging** instead of wheels, which runs smoothly over snow
sleep	1. a rest in which you lose any **sleeping** sense of the things about **sleepless** you **sleepy** 2. to rest your body by sleep- **slept** ing: to be asleep
sleeper	1. someone who is sleeping 2. a heavy piece of wood or concrete to which railway lines are fastened
sleet	snow or hail falling with rain
sleeve	the part of your clothes which covers your arm
slice	1. a thin, flat piece which is **sliced** cut off something **slicing** 2. to cut anything in slices

slide
1. a hair clip
2. to slip along over something smooth, such as ice — **slid** **sliding**

slight
1. not big — **slightly**
2. not important

slim — not fat — **slimmer** **slimmest**

slime — very fine slippery mud — **slimy**

slip
1. a small mistake — **slipped**
2. to slide a little way by accident — **slippery** **slipping**
3. to go quietly and quickly

slippers — soft comfortable shoes to wear indoors

slit
1. a long thin cut or opening in anything — **slitting**
2. to make a long cut in something

slope — slanting ground — **sloped** **sloping**

slot — a narrow opening or groove in something — **slot-machine**

slow
1. behind in time — **slowed**
2. taking a long time to do something — **slower** **slowest** **slowing** **slowly**

slush
1. soft mud — **slushy**
2. half-melted snow

sly — cunning: crafty — **slyly**

smack
1. a quick blow from an open hand — **smacked**
2. to slap anyone with the flat part of your hand — **smacking**

small — little in size or amount: not large — **smaller** **smallest**

smart
1. well-dressed — **smarted**
2. quick and sharp — **smarter**
3. to feel a sharp, tingling pain — **smartest** **smarting** **smartly**

smash
1. a collision: a crash
2. to dash something to pieces

smashes
smashed
smashes
smashing

smell
1. the scent of anything
2. to notice the scent of any- thing
3. to have a scent

smelling
smelly
smelt

smile
1. a happy look
2. to look pleased and happy

smiled
smiling

smog   smoke and fog together

smoke
1. the fumes that come from something burning
2. to give out smoke
3. to use a cigarette, pipe or cigar

smoked
smoker
smoking
smoky

smooth
1. without any roughness: level
2. to make something level and smooth

smoothed
smoother
smoothest
smoothing
smoothly

smudge
1. a smear: a dirty mark
2. to make a dirty mark on something

smudged
smudging
smudgy

smuggle   to take goods into or out of a country in secret, to avoid paying a tax on them

smuggled
smuggler
smuggling

snail   a little creature, with a shell on its back, which crawls very slowly

snake   an animal like a large worm

snap
1. a sudden sharp or cracking sound
2. to break suddenly
3. to try to bite something or somebody
4. to speak sharply and angrily

snapped
snappily
snapping
snappy
snapshot

snatch   to grab something quickly

snatched
snatches
snatching

sneeze	the sudden noise you make when something tickles your nose	**sneezed** **sneezing**
sniff	to breathe air in quickly through your nose	**sniffed** **sniffing**
snore	to breathe noisily while you are asleep	**snored** **snoring**
snow	1. soft white flakes of frozen rain, which sometimes fall on a cold day 2. to fall as snow	**snowball** **snowbound** **snowed** **snowflake** **snowing** **snowman** **snowstorm** **snowy**
soak	1. to leave something lying in liquid 2. to make something very wet	**soaked** **soaking**
soap	something made from fat and used for washing	**soap-powder** **soapsuds** **soapy**
soccer	football played with a round ball	
sock	a short stocking: a covering for the foot and ankle	
sofa	a long, soft seat with a back and arms, on which two or three people can sit	
soft	1. not hard 2. easily bent or squashed 3. gentle and quiet	**softer** **softest** **softly**
soil	1. the ground in which plants grow 2. to make something dirty	**soiled** **soiling**
sold	(My mother *sold* a book for 5p)	
soldier	a person in the army	

sole	1. the bottom of your foot	**soled**
	2. the bottom part of a shoe	**soling**
	3. a flat fish which can be eaten	
	4. only	
solid	1. firm and not changing its shape	
	2. not hollow	
solve	to work out the answer to a problem	**solution** **solved** **solving**
some	an amount	**somebody** **someone** **something** **sometimes** **somewhere**
somersault	to turn head over heels	**somer-** **saulted** **somer-** **saulting**
son	the boy child of a mother and father	
song	1. words set to music	
	2. sweet sounds made by a bird	
soon	before long: shortly	**sooner** **soonest**
soot	specks of partly burnt coal which smoke leaves in a chimney	**sooty**
sore	1. a painful spot on your skin	**soreness**
	2. tender and painful	
sorrow	sadness	**sorrowful**
sorry	sad because you have done wrong, or because of something that has happened: regretful	
sort	1. a kind	**sorted**
	2. to separate things into groups	**sorting**

sought	(John *sought* his toys but could not find them)	
soul	the part of a person that is thought to live on after death	
sound	1. something that we can hear 2. in a good state: healthy 3. to make a noise	**sounded** **sounding** **sound-proof**
soup	liquid food made by boiling vegetables or meat	
sour	an unripe, acid taste	
source	the place where a river or stream starts	
south	the opposite to north	**southern**
souvenir	a thing kept to remind you of a person or a place	
sow	1. a female pig 2. to plant seeds	**sowed** **sowing** **sown**
space	1. the distance between things 2. far from the earth, where there is no air	**space-ship**
spade	a sharp-edged blade on a handle, used for digging	
span	the distance between the tips of your thumb and little finger when your hand is stretched out	
spaniel	a long-eared dog with a silky coat	
spanner	a tool for turning bolts or nuts	
spare	extra: not needed	
spark	a tiny piece thrown out from something burning: a flash	**sparking**
sparkle	to glitter or glisten	**sparkled** **sparkler** **sparkling**
sparrow	a small brownish-grey bird	
speak	to talk	**speaker** **speaking** **spoke**

spear	a weapon with a long handle and a sharp-pointed end	
special	for a particular use	**specialist** **specially**
speck	a tiny piece, often of dirt	**speckled**
spectacles	glasses worn to help your sight	
spectator	someone who watches a show, a game or anything happening	
speech	1. a talk to an audience 2. the power to speak	**speeches** **speechless**
speed	1. the rate at which something moves 2. quickness 3. to move very fast	**speeded** **speeding** **speedy**
speedometer	an instrument in a car to show how fast it is travelling	
speedway	a race-track for motor-cycles or cars	
spell	1. words supposed to have magic power 2. to arrange letters to make words	**spelled** **spelling** **spelt**
spend	1. to pay out money 2. to use up time in doing something	**spending** **spent**
sphere	a ball shape	**spherical**
spice	something like pepper or curry, for making food more tasty	
spider	a creature with eight legs, which spins a web to catch insects	
spill	to tip over	**spilled** **spilling** **spilt**
spin	1. to twist into threads 2. to turn round and round	**spinning** **spun**
spiral	a screw-shaped curve	

spite	trying to hurt someone by cruel words or behaviour	**spiteful** **spitefully**
splash	to scatter water about	**splashed** **splashes** **splashing**
splash-down	to land in the water, as some space capsules do	
splendid	gorgeous: magnificent: showy	**splendidly**
splinter	a sharp piece broken off something	**splintered**
split	1. a long tear or crack 2. to tear or break something	**splitting**
spoil	to damage or destroy something	**spoiled** **spoiling** **spoilt**
spoke	1. a bar or strong wire which holds the rim of a wheel to the centre 2. (When the teacher *spoke* we all listened)	**spoken**
sponge	1. a soft thing which soaks up water and is used in the bath 2. to wash or wipe something with a sponge	**sponged** **sponging** **spongy**
spoon	something used for eating or stirring soft food	**spoonful**
sport	a game such as football, racing or fishing	**sports- jacket** **sportsman**
spot	1. a stain or mark 2. to see something	**spotless** **spotted** **spotter** **spotting**
spout	a tube with a shaped mouth-piece for liquid to run through	
sprain	1. a twisted muscle 2. to harm a muscle by twisting it	**sprained** **spraining**
sprang	(The tiger *sprang* out from its hiding-place)	

spray	1. a shower of tiny drops of water 2. to shoot a liquid out from anything, in a shower	**sprayed** **sprayer** **spraying**
spread	to make something cover a greater surface, by unrolling, smearing or flattening it out	**spreading**
spring	1. water flowing out from the ground 2. a coil of metal which goes back into shape after it has been bent or pressed 3. to jump or leap	**sprang** **springing** **sprung**
spring	the season between winter and summer	
sprinkle	to scatter lightly	**sprinkled** **sprinkling**
sprint	to run as fast as you can for a short distance	**sprinted** **sprinter** **sprinting**
spun	(The spider *spun* its web and caught a fly)	
spy	1. someone who secretly watches an enemy 2. to watch secretly	**spies** **spied** **spies** **spy-catcher** **spying**
squabble	to quarrel noisily	**squabbled** **squabbling**
square	1. a shape with four straight, equal sides and four equal angles 2. an open space in a town	
squash	1. a fruit drink 2. to squeeze or crush	squashes **squashed** **squashes** **squashing**
squeak	to make a short, sharp, high sound	**squeaked** **squeaking**
squeal	to make a long sharp cry, usually of pain or fright	**squealed** **squealing**

squeeze	to press or crush	**squeezed** **squeezing**
squirrel	a small animal with a bushy tail	
squirt	to shoot water out in a thin stream	**squirted** **squirter** **squirting**
stab	to wound someone with a pointed weapon	**stabbed** **stabbing**
stable	a shelter for a horse	
stack	1. a pile of things one on top of another 2. to make a pile of things	**stacked** **stacking**
staff	1. a strong stick 2. a number of people who work together, as in a school or office	**staff-room**
stag	a male deer	
stage	the platform on which plays are acted	
stagger	to walk in a very unsteady way	**staggered** **staggering**
stain	1. a dirty mark not easy to remove 2. a dye for wood	**stained** **staining** **stainless**
stairs	a number of steps	**staircase**
stake	a post fixed in the ground	
stale	not fresh: old	
stalk	1. the stem of a flower or plant 2. to follow an animal in order to catch or watch it	**stalked** **stalking**
stall	1. a shop in a market 2. a seat near the stage in a theatre	
stamp	1. a piece of paper to stick on letters or parcels so that you can send them by post 2. to stick on a stamp 3. to bang your foot on the ground	**stamped** **stamping**

stand	1. raised seats, usually under cover, from which people watch a game or races 2. to be upright on your feet 3. to suffer without complaining	**standing** **stood**
star	1. a large object in space, seen as a point of light in the sky at night 2. a famous actor or actress	
starch	1. a white powder used with water for stiffening clothes 2. to stiffen clothes with starch	**starched** **starches** **starching** **starchy**
stare	to look hard at anything with wide-open eyes	**stared** **staring**
starling	a bird with dark, speckled feathers	
start	to begin	**started** **starter** **starting**
starve	to suffer or die because of lack of food	**starvation** **starved** **starving**
station	1. a place where trains or 'buses stop 2. a building for police officers or fire fighters	
stationary	standing still	
stationery	materials for writing	
statue	a carving in wood or stone, usually of a person or an animal	
stay	to stop in one place for a time	**stayed** **staying**
steady	1. firm: not rocking or moving 2. (Joan is a *steady* worker. She is neither fast nor slow)	**steadily**
steak	a thick slice of meat	

steal	to take something which is not yours	**stealing** **stole** **stolen**
steam	1. the cloud you see coming from boiling water 2. to give off steam	**steamed** **steaming**
steamer	a ship driven by steam	
steel	a very strong metal made from iron	
steep	sloping very sharply	**steeper** **steepest** **steeply**
steeple	a pointed tower	
steer	to guide anything	**steered** **steering**
stem	a stalk	
step	1. one pace with your foot 2. one part of a staircase 3. to take one pace	**stepped** **stepping**
stern	1. the back end of a ship 2. strict: severe	
stew	1. a dish of vegetables and meat, which have been cooked together in water 2. to cook something slowly in boiling water	**stewed** **stewing**
stick	1. a thin bit of wood 2. to fix something with paste or glue	**sticking** **sticky** **stuck**
stiff	1. cannot be bent easily 2. hard or difficult	**stiffen** **stiffly** **stiffness**
stile	a fence with a step on each side	
still	1. not moving 2. in spite of something: yet	
stilt	a pole with a step at the side, used in pairs for walking above the ground	

sting	1. a small amount of poison pricked into your skin by an insect or plant 2. the part of an insect or plant that causes a sting 3. to prick a small amount of poison into the skin	**stinging** **stung**
stir	1. to mix something, usually with a spoon 2. to move	**stirred** **stirring**
stitch	1. a thread put through cloth with a needle, or a loop made with wool in knitting 2. to sew with thread	stitches **stitched** stitches **stitching**
stocking	a covering for the foot and leg, usually made of nylon	
stoke	to put fuel on a fire	**stoked** **stoker** **stoking**
stole	(The thief *stole* the money from the shop)	**stolen**
stomach	the part of the body where food is partly dissolved	
stone	a piece of rock: a pebble	
stood	(We *stood* at the roadside to watch the carnival go by)	
stool	a small seat without a back or arms	
stoop	to bend the body forward	**stooped** **stooping**
stop	1. a stopping place 2. to bring someone or something to a standstill 3. to halt: to end	**stoppage** **stopped** **stopping**
stopper	a plug or cork for a bottle	
store	1. a place where things can be kept until they are wanted 2. a large shop selling many different things 3. to put a thing away until it is needed	**stored** **storing**

storey	a floor of a building, and the rooms in it	
stork	a bird with a long beak, legs and neck	
storm	very bad weather with heavy rain, strong winds, thunder and lightning or snow	**stormy**
story	a tale	**stories**
stout	1. strongly built 2. fat	
stove	a closed-in fire for cooking, or for warming a building	
stowaway	someone who hides in a ship or aircraft, so that he can travel without paying his fare	
straight	1. without a curve or bend 2. honest	**straighten** **straighter** **straightest**
strain	1. to try very hard to do a diffi-cult thing 2. to pull or stretch	**strained** **straining**
strait	a narrow channel of sea	
strange	1. new or not known to you 2. unusual	**strangely** **stranger** **strangest**
stranger	1. someone you do not know 2. a person in a country or town to which he does not belong	
strap	1. a strip of leather or cloth with a buckle 2. to fasten with straps	**strapped** **strapping**
straw	dry stalks of cut corn	
strawberry	a soft, juicy, red fruit, with small yellow seeds on its skin	**strawberries**
stray	to wander from home or lose your way	**strayed** **straying**
stream	a brook: a small river	
stream-lined	smoothly shaped to pass smoothly through air or water	

street	a road with houses or shops	
strength	being strong: power	
stretch	to pull out to make something longer	**stretched** **stretches** **stretching**
stretcher	a canvas bed for carrying any-one who is ill or injured	
strict	stern	**stricter** **strictest**
strike	1. a time when a group of people try to get something they want by refusing to work 2. to hit	**striking** **struck**
string	fine cord: twine	**stringy**
strip	1. a thin, long piece of any-thing 2. to take the cover off some-thing	**stripped** **stripping**
stripe	a narrow band of colour	**striped**
stroke	1. a movement of the arm 2. a swimming movement 3. to smooth something with the hand	**stroked** **stroking**
stroll	1. a slow pleasant walk 2. to go for a slow walk	**strolled** **strolling**
strong	1. powerful 2. tough: hard to break 3. healthy	**stronger** **strongest** **strongly**
struck	(I cut my head when I *struck* it against the wall)	
struggle	1. to fight with something or someone 2. to try hard	**struggled** **struggling**
stubborn	hard to persuade: unwilling	
stuck	1. glued or pasted 2. not free	
stud	1. a double-headed button for holding a collar in place 2. a nail with a large knob	

study	1. a room for quiet work 2. to read to learn	**studies** **student** **studied** **studies** **studying**
stuff	1. material that anything is made from 2. to fill something tightly	
stuffy	short of fresh air	
stumble	to catch your foot on something and lose your balance	**stumbled** **stumbling**
stump	1. the part of the tree still in the ground after the tree has been cut down 2. one of three wooden sticks which make a wicket for cricket	**stumped** **stumping**
stung	(John screamed when he was *stung* by a wasp)	
stupid	silly: foolish: dull	**stupidity** **stupidly**
stutter	to stumble over words while trying to speak: to stammer	**stuttered** **stuttering**
sty	1. the building where a pig is kept 2. a painful swelling on an eyelid	**sties** or **styes**
subject	1. the thing you write, read and learn about 2. a person ruled by a king or queen	
submarine	a warship that can sail both above and below the surface of the sea	
submerge	to go down under the water	**submerged** **submerging**
subtract	to take away	**subtracted** **subtraction**
suburb	a district on the edge of a town or city	**suburban**

subway	a passageway under a busy road	
succeed	1. to do well at what you set out to do 2. to come after, and take the place of, somebody	**succeeded** **succeeding** **succession**
success	a thing or person that turns out well	**successes** **successful**
such	(It was *such* a beautiful day that we went swimming)	
suck	to draw something into your mouth	**sucked** **sucking**
sudden	happening quickly and without warning	**suddenly**
suet	solid fat of cattle or sheep used in cooking	
suffer	to feel pain or sorrow	**suffered** **suffering**
sufficient	enough	
sugar	something used to sweeten food	
suggest	to offer someone an idea or plan	**suggested** **suggesting** **suggestion**
suit	1. a set of matching clothes 2. to fit in with your ideas or wishes 3. to go well with someone's looks or colouring	**suited** **suiting**
suitable	just right	**suitability**
sulk	to show you are cross by refusing to speak to people	**sulked** **sulking** **sulky**
sultana	one kind of grape that has been partly dried and is used in cakes	
summer	the season between spring and autumn	

summit	the top, usually of a mountain	
sun	the star that gives us light and warmth	**sunburnt** **sunflower** **sunlight** **sunny** **sunrise** **sunset** **sunshine** **sunstroke**
Sunday	the first day of the week	
sung	(The song was *sung* well)	
sunk	(The ship was *sunk* when it hit the rocks)	
supermarket	a large shop where customers usually serve themselves, and pay as they leave	
supersonic	travelling faster than sound	
supper	the last meal of the day	
support	1. anything which helps to hold something up or which bears a mass (weight) 2. to hold something up	**supported** **supporter** **supporting**
suppose	to accept as likely	**supposed** **supposing**
sure	certain: without any doubts	
surf	large waves breaking on the shore	
surface	the top or outside of something	
surgery	the room where a doctor sees her patients	**surgeries**
surname	your family name	
surprise	1. something unexpected 2. to give someone a surprise	**surprised** **surprising**
surrender	to give up	**surrendered** **surrendering**
surround	to be all round something or someone	**surrounded** **surrounding**

suspect	1. someone who is believed to have done something wrong 2. to have a feeling that someone has done something wrong	**suspected** **suspecting**
suspicious	1. doubting whether something is true: not trusting 2. not to be trusted	**suspiciously**
swallow	1. a bird with pointed wings and a forked tail 2. to let something pass down your throat	**swallowed** **swallowing**
swam	(The sailor *swam* to the raft)	
swamp	a boggy piece of land	**swamped** **swamping** **swampy**
swan	a large, white bird with a very long neck	
swarm	a crowd of bees, all close together	**swarmed** **swarming**
sway	to rock from side to side	**swayed** **swaying**
swear	1. to take an oath 2. to use bad language	**swearing** **swore** **sworn**
sweat	1. the wetness that comes on your skin when you are hot 2. to become wet through being hot	**sweated** **sweating**
sweater	a woollen jersey or pullover	
sweep	1. a person who sweeps chimneys 2. to use a brush or broom	**sweeper** **sweeping** **swept**
sweet	1. (I buy *sweets* with my pocket money) 2. with a sugary taste 3. pleasant to hear or see	**sweeter** **sweetest** **sweetly**
swell	1. to get bigger 2. to get louder	**swelled** **swelling** **swollen**

swept	(Jim *swept* up all the dust from the floor)	
swerve	to turn to one side suddenly	**swerved** **swerving**
swift	1. a bird like a swallow 2. quick	**swifter** **swiftest** **swiftly**
swim	to move through water, using your arms and legs	**swam** **swimmer** **swimming** **swum**
swing	1. a seat hanging from ropes 2. to move backwards and forwards in a curve	**swinging** **swung**
switch	1. a thing for turning electricity on or off 2. to use a switch for turning electricity on or off 3. to change over	**switches** **switched** **switches** **switching**
swollen	(My leg was *swollen* where it had been hit)	
swoop	to dive downwards	**swooped** **swooping**
sword	a sharp-pointed weapon with a long, thin blade	
swore	(I *swore* to keep the secret)	
sworn	(The robber had *sworn* to get her revenge)	
swung	(The monkey *swung* from one branch to another)	
sycamore	a tree with broad five-pointed leaves	
symmetry	having the two halves the same shape and size	**symmetric** **symmetrical**
syrup	a sugary liquid	

t

table
a piece of furniture with a flat surface which stands on legs
tablecloth
tablespoon

tack
1. a long loose sewing-stitch
2. a short, flat-topped nail
3. to fasten something down with a tack or tacking-stitch
tacked
tacking

tackle
1. to try to do something that is awkward
2. to try to get the ball away from another player in a game
tackled
tackling

tadpole
a partly-grown toad, frog or newt

tail
the part which hangs or sticks out from the back of an animal

tailor
a person who makes suits, coats and trousers

take
1. to get hold of: to receive
2. (I *take* my satchel home at night)
taken
taking
took

tale
a story

talk
1. a speech
2. to speak
talkative
talked
talking

tall
high
taller
tallest

tame
1. not wild or fierce
2. to make obedient
tamed
tamely
tamer
tamest
taming

tangerine
a kind of small orange

tangle
twisted together in a muddle

tank
1. a large holder for liquids or gases
2. an armoured car with tracks instead of wheels

tanker a ship for carrying oil or other liquids

tap
1. a pipe or hole which can be **tapped** opened or closed to let **tapping** liquid through
2. to hit gently

tape a narrow strip of material, usually cloth

taper to get thinner towards the end **tapered** **tapering**

tape recorder a machine that records and plays back sound

tar
1. a dark-coloured sticky **tarred** liquid, taken from coal or **tarring** wood
2. to put tar on

target something to aim at

tart
1. a pie with fruit in it, or pastry with jam on it
2. sour in taste

tartan woollen cloth with a checked pattern

task a piece of work to be done

taste
1. the flavour of food **tasted**
2. to notice the flavour of any- **tasteless** thing put in your mouth **tasting** **tasty**

taught (We are *taught* by a teacher)

tax money paid to the govern- **taxes** ment

taxi a car for hiring

tea a drink made from the young **teapot** leaves of the tea plant **teaspoon** **teaspoonful**

teach to explain how to do some- **taught** thing: to give lessons **teacher** **teaches** **teaching**

team a number of people, or animals, working together

tear	1. a drop of salty water from your eye 2. to rip	**tearing** **tore** **torn**
tease	to annoy somebody in fun	**teased** **teasing**
teeth	(We clean our *teeth* after meals)	
telegram	a written message sent very quickly by the Post Office in the past	
telephone	an electrical instrument by means of which sounds are carried by wires over long distances	
telescope	an eye-glass which makes far away things seem near	
television	the sending and receiving of pictures by radio	
tell	to say a message or story to someone	**telling** **told**
temper	1. the sort of mood you are in 2. anger	
temperature	the reading on a thermometer which shows how hot or cold anything is	
tempt	to try to get someone to do something which they ought not to do	**temptation** **tempted** **tempting**
ten	10	**tenth**
tender	1. a railway truck which carries fuel and water for the locomotive 2. soft: not tough 3. loving	
tennis	a game for two or four people, played with rackets and a ball	
tent	a canvas shelter	
term	the time spent in school between holidays	

terminus	the place where a 'bus or train ends its journey	**termini**
terrier	a small dog	
terrify	to fill someone with terror	**terrific** **terrified** **terrifies** **terrifying**
terror	great fear and dread	**terrible** **terribly**
test	1. an examination 2. to try out someone or something	**tested** **testing**
than	(Four is bigger *than* three)	
thank	to say you are grateful	**thanked** **thankful** **thankfully** **thanking**
that	1. (He knows *that* I will be late) 2. (This is the one *that* I like)	
thatch	a roof of straw or reeds	**thatches** **thatched** **thatching**
thaw	to melt from snow or ice	**thawed** **thawing**
theatre	a place where people watch actors on a stage	
their	belonging to them	
them	(Sally and John were good, so the teacher gave *them* a star)	**themselves**
then	1. at that time 2. so after that	
there	in that place	**therefore**
thermometer	an instrument for measuring how hot or cold anything is	
thermos	a special flask that keeps what it holds hot or cold	
these	(*These* books are mine)	

they	(John and Mary were late so *they* ran home)	
thick	1. wide: not thin 2. crowded 3. dense 4. not runny	**thickly** **thickness**
thief	someone who steals	**thieves**
thigh	the top of your leg	
thimble	a finger cover, to help to press a needle through cloth	
thin	not thick: slim	**thinly** **thinner** **thinnest**
thing	any object	
think	1. to use your mind 2. to believe	**thinking** **thought**
third	3rd	
thirst	the feeling you have when you want a drink	**thirsty**
thirteen	13	**thirteenth**
thirty	30	**thirtieth**
this	(*This* pen is better than that one)	
thistle	a plant with prickly leaves and a purple, white or yellow flower	
thorn	the prickle of a bush, plant or tree	**thorny**
those	(*Those* pencils over there have been sharpened)	
thorough	careful: well done	**thoroughly**
though	even if	
thought	1. an idea: something which you think 2. (I *thought* I had finished my work)	**thoughtful** **thoughtless**
thousand	1000	**thousandth**

thread	1. a piece of cotton, wool, nylon, or silk cord, or any fibre 2. to push thread through a hole in anything	**threaded** **threading**
threat	a warning that trouble is coming	
threaten	to say that you will hurt or punish someone	**threatened** **threatening**
three	3	**third**
threw	(Jill *threw* the ball into the air, and John caught it)	
thrill	1. an excited feeling 2. to make someone feel excited	**thrilled** **thrilling**
thriller	an exciting story, usually about crime	
throat	the tube which leads from mouth to stomach	
throb	to beat strongly	**throbbed** **throbbing**
throne	a special chair for a king or queen, or very important person	
through	from one end to the other	
throw	to fling something through the air	**threw** **throwing** **thrown**
thrush	a brown bird with a sweet song	**thrushes**
thud	a dull, bumping sound	
thumb	the short, thick finger, nearest the wrist	
thump	to beat with the fist	**thumped** **thumping**
thunder	the loud noise that follows lightning	**thunder-** **storm** **thundery**
Thursday	the fifth day of the week	

tick	1. the clicking sound made by a clock 2. a mark to show that your work has been checked	**ticked** **ticking**
ticket	a card giving you the right to a place on a 'bus or train or to watch something	
tickle	to touch someone lightly to make him laugh	**tickled** **tickling** **ticklish**
tide	the rise and fall of the sea twice daily	
tidy	1. neat 2. to arrange anything neatly	**tidied** **tidier** **tidies** **tidiest** **tidily** **tidiness** **tidying**
tie	1. a band round the neck, which ties in front 2. to fasten with string or ribbon 3. to have the same score	**tied** **ties** **tying**
tiger	a large, striped animal like a fierce cat	**tigress**
tight	fitting closely	**tighter** **tightest** **tightly** **tights**
tile	a thin slab, usually made of baked clay	**tiled**
till	1. a money-drawer in a shop 2. up to: as late as 3. to dig land	**tilled**
tilt	to slope or slant anything	**tilted** **tilting**
timber	wood	
time	1. the hour of the day 2. to find out how long it takes to do something 3. (We had a good *time* today)	**timed** **timetable** **timing**

timid	shy: easily made afraid	**timidly**
tingle	to have a prickling or stinging feeling	**tingled** **tingling**
tinned	in a sealed tin	
tinsel	shiny metal threads or strips used for decoration	
tiny	very small	**tinier** **tiniest**
tip	1. the pointed end of anything 2. a small gift of money given to someone who has been helpful 3. to tilt: to overturn	**tipped** **tipping**
tiptoe	to walk on your toes	**tiptoed** **tiptoeing**
tire	to make weary	**tired** **tiring**
tissue	a very thin, soft paper	
title	1. the name of anything which is written 2. a name to show a person's rank	**titled**
toad	a creature like a frog, but with a drier skin	
toast	1. bread browned by heat 2. to make bread brown by heating it	**toasted** **toaster** **toasting**
tobacco	the leaves of the tobacco plant which are used for smoking	**tobacconist**
toboggan	a sledge for sliding on snow	
today	this day	
toe	one of the five tips of the foot	
toffee	a sweet made from butter, sugar and treacle	
together	1. with something or someone else 2. at the same time	
toilet	a lavatory or wash place	
told	(I *told* him to sit)	

tomato	a soft fruit with a red skin	**tomatoes**
tomorrow	the day after today	
tongs	a kind of pincer, used for picking up coal	
tongue	the loose piece of flesh in the mouth which helps you to eat and speak	
tonight	after this evening	
tonsils	two glands at the back of the mouth to protect the throat	**tonsillitis**
too	1. also 2. more than enough	
took	(Eric *took* a present to his friend)	
tool	something to work with	
tooth	a bone which grows in your jaw for biting and chewing	**teeth** **toothache**
torch	a light carried in the hand	**torches**
tore	(Jane *tore* her dress on a nail)	
torn	(Jane's dress was *torn* by a nail)	
tortoise	a reptile, with a hard shell, which moves very slowly	
torture	to be cruel to someone by causing great pain	**tortured** **torturing**
toss	to throw into the air	**tossed** **tosses** **tossing**
total	1. the complete amount 2. complete 3. to add up to	**totalled** **totalling**
touch	1. to feel 2. to be so near that there is no space between	**touched** **touches** **touching**
tough	hard to break or cut	
tow	to pull along	**towed** **towing**
towards	in the direction of	

towel	a thick cotton or linen cloth for drying your body
tower	a tall, narrow building
town	a large number of houses and other buildings
toy	something to play with

trace
1. a mark left behind
2. to copy something by following its shape on thin paper that is placed over it

traced
tracing

track
1. marks left by someone or something as he or it passed
2. a rough path
3. railway lines
4. to follow a track

tracked
tracking

tractor a powerful machine used on farms for pulling heavy loads

trade
1. buying and selling things
2. a job needing skilled hands
3. to buy and sell things

traded
tradesman
trading

traffic people or goods coming and going by road, rail, sea or air

trail
1. a track left by something as it passed by
2. to drag something along

trailed
trailer
trailing

train
1. railway carriages drawn by an engine
2. to prepare by practising

trained
trainer
training

traitor someone who betrays his friends or his country

tramp a wandering beggar

transfer
1. a picture or pattern you can stick on to something else
2. to move something or somebody to another place

transferred
transferring

transfusion passing blood from one person to another

transistor
1. a thing used to increase an electrical current
2. a portable radio

transparent	letting light pass through	**transparency**
transplant	to take up or out and plant in another place	**transplanted transplanting**
trap	1. (I set a *trap* to catch mice) 2. a two-wheeled, open carriage 3. to catch a person or animal, usually by a trick	**trapped trapping**
trapdoor	a door in a floor, stage or ceiling	
travel	to make a journey	**travelled traveller travelling**
trawler	a fishing boat which drags its net	
tray	a flat board with raised edges	
treacle	syrup made from sugar	
tread	to walk	**treading trod trodden**
treason	betraying your country	
treasure	something worth a great deal of money	**treasurer treasury**
treat	1. anything that gives you much pleasure 2. to look after	**treated treating treatment**
tree	a large plant with a thick wood stem and branches	
tremble	to shiver with fear or excitement	**trembled trembling**
trench	a long narrow ditch, dug in the ground	**trenches**
trespass	to go on someone else's property without permission	**trespassed trespasser trespassing**

trial	a way of testing something or somebody	
triangle	1. the shape made by joining three straight lines 2. a musical percussion instrument	
trick	1. a clever or funny act 2. to cheat	**tricked** **tricking** **tricky**
trickle	to flow in a thin stream	**trickle** **trickling**
tricycle	a three-wheeled cycle	
tried	(Peter *tried* on his new boots)	
trifle	1. a sweet mixture of sponge cake, fruit or jam, custard and cream 2. something that is not worth much	
trigger	the part of a gun which you pull in order to fire the bullet	
trim	1. neat: tidy 2. to cut the rough edges off something	**trimmed** **trimming**
trip	1. an outing 2. to stumble 3. to move lightly	**tripped** **tripper** **tripping**
trod	(I slipped when I *trod* on the ice)	
trodden	(The flowers were *trodden* down by the stray horses)	
trolley	a hand-drawn cart	
trolley-bus	a 'bus that is driven by electricity from overhead wires	**trolley-** **buses**
trot	to run slowly	**trotted** **trotting**
trombone	a musical wind instrument	
trouble	worry: difficulty	**troublesome**
trousers	a piece of clothing with two legs to cover the body from the waist to the ankles	

trowel	1. a small spade-shaped tool used by a gardener 2. a flat-bladed tool used by a bricklayer	
truant	someone who is away from school without permission	
truck	1. a railway wagon 2. a lorry	
true	1. correct 2. real 3. faithful	**truly** **truth** **truthful** **truthfully**
trumpet	a musical wind instrument	
truncheon	a short club which a policeman sometimes carries	
trunk	1. the thick part of a tree or body 2. a large luggage box 3. the long nose of an elephant	
trust	to believe without question	**trusted** **trusting**
try	1. to give something a trial 2. to attempt	**tried** **tries** **trying**
tube	1. a long, narrow pipe 2. the underground railway in London	
tuck	1. a sewn fold in material 2. to cover snugly in bed	**tucked** **tucking**
Tuesday	the third day of the week	
tug	1. a boat used for towing 2. to pull with a jerk	**tugged** **tugging**
tulip	a plant grown from a bulb, with a flower like a small cup	
tumble	1. a sudden fall 2. to fall	**tumbled** **tumbling**
tumbler	a drinking glass	
tune	1. the music of a song 2. to make a musical instrument give the right sound	**tuned** **tuning**

tunic	1. a dress worn in school 2. the jacket part of a uniform	
tunnel	a passage cut through a hill or under the ground	
turban	a long piece of cloth worn wrapped around the head	
turf	surface soil thickly planted with short grass	
turkey	a large farmyard bird, usually eaten at Christmas	
turn	1. to move round 2. to change direction or position	**turned** **turning**
turnip	a plant with a round white root which is eaten as a vegetable	
turnstile	a gate which turns on a centre pole and which allows one person at a time to pass through it	
tusk	a very long tooth, sticking out beyond the mouth	
twelve	12	**twelfth**
twenty	20	**twentieth**
twice	two times: double	
twig	a very small branch	
twin	one of two children in a family born at the same time	
twinkle	to throw out gleams of light: to sparkle	**twinkled** **twinkling**
twist	to turn round and round	**twisted** **twisting**
two	2	
tying	(Sally was *tying* up her shoelace)	
typewriter	a machine with keys worked by the fingers, for writing	

typhoon a very bad storm

tyre a rubber band put round a wheel

u

ugly not pleasant to look at **uglier**
ugliest
ugliness

ukulele a musical instrument like a guitar

umbrella a round frame covered with waterproof cloth, which you use for sheltering from the rain

umpire someone who is in charge of a game and sees that you keep to the rules

unable not able to do something

unarmed having no weapons

unbeaten never defeated

unbolt to move back the bolt on a door or gate **unbolted**
unbolting

unbutton to undo a button **unbuttoned**
unbuttoning

uncertain not sure

uncle your mother's or your father's brother, or your aunt's husband

uncomfortable uneasy: not comfortable

uncommon unusual

unconscious not knowing what is going on around you

uncork to take the cork out of a bottle **uncorked**
uncorking

uncover to take the cover off something **uncovered**
uncovering

undamaged not hurt or broken in any way

undecided when you have not made up your mind

under below   **underneath**

underground 1. a railway that runs under the ground
2. under the ground

undergrowth thick, low-growing bushes

underhand secret: sly

underline to put a line under something   **underlined**
underlining

understand to know what something means   **understand-**
ing
understood

undo to untie or unfasten   **undid**
undoes
undoing

undress to take clothes off   **undressed**
undresses
undressing

uneasy worried: anxious: uncomfortable

unemployed out of work

uneven rough: not level

unfair not just: not fair

unfasten to undo or untie something   **unfastened**
unfastening

unfit 1. not well   2. not suitable

unfold to spread or open out   **unfolded**
unfolding

unfortunate unlucky   **unfortun-**
ately

ungrateful not thankful

unhappy sad: miserable   **unhappily**

unhealthy not well: in poor health

uniform clothes worn by people who belong to a school or a special group

universe everything that there is   **universal**

university	a school for higher education	**universities**
unkind	cruel: not kind	
unless	(You will not learn *unless* you try hard)	
unload	to take a load off something	**unloaded** **unloading**
unlock	to open a lock	**unlocked** **unlocking**
unlucky	out of luck	
unnecessary	not needed	
unnoticed	not seen	
unpack	to take the things out of a case or parcel	**unpacked** **unpacking**
unpleasant	not pleasing	
unpopular	not well liked	
unroll	to open out a roll of something	**unrolled** **unrolling**
untie	to unfasten a knot	**untied** **untying**
until	till	
unusual	not very common: rare	
unwrap	to take the cover off a parcel	**unwrapped** **unwrapping**
upon	on	
upright	standing straight up	
uproar	a great noise of shouting	
upset	to overturn or disturb	**upsetting**
upstairs	on the next floor up	
urgent	needing to be dealt with at once	**urgently**
use	1. (My friend gave me the *use* of his pen) 2. (John and Mary *use* their bicycles for the journey to school)	**useful** **useless**
usual	ordinary: common	**usually**

V

vacuum	a space with no air in it	
vain	too proud of yourself: conceited	
valley	a strip of low land between hills	
valuable	worth a great deal	
vanish	to disappear	**vanished** **vanishes** **vanishing**
various	different sorts	
varnish	1. a sticky liquid which gives a hard, shiny surface to things 2. to put varnish on to something	**varnishes** **varnished** **varnishes** **varnishing**
vase	a jar to hold flowers	
vaseline	a greasy ointment	
vast	very large	
veal	the meat from a calf	
vegetable	a plant used for food	
veil	a net covering for a woman's face	
vein	one of the tubes in the body which carry blood	
velvet	a smooth, soft, silky cloth	
verdict	judgement: decision	
verse	lines of poetry	
versus	against	
vertical	exactly upright	**vertically**
very	true: really	
vessel	1. a boat or ship 2. something to hold liquids	
vest	a garment worn next to the skin	
vex	to annoy	**vexed** **vexes** **vexing**

vicar	a Church of England parson in charge of a small district	**vicarage**
vicious	1. spiteful 2. wicked	
victory	a win	**victories** **victorious**
view	what you can see	
village	a small group of houses in the country	**villagers**
villain	an evil person	
vine	the plant on which grapes grow	**vineyard**
vinegar	a sour liquid used for pickling and to flavour food	**vinegary**
violet	1. a bluish-purple colour 2. a plant which has flowers of a bluish-purple colour	
violin	a four-stringed musical instrument played with a bow	**violinist**
visit	to call and see someone	**visited** **visiting** **visitor**
voice	you use it to talk or sing	
volcano	a mountain that is made when molten rock and ash are forced out through a hole in the earth's crust	**volcanoes**
volume	1. a book 2. the amount of space taken up by anything	
vote	to choose someone at an election	**voted** **voter** **voting**
voyage	a long journey by sea	
vulture	a large bird that feeds on dead animals	

W

wade	to walk through water	**waded** **wader** **wading**
wafer	a very thin biscuit	
wage	money earned by working	
wagon **(waggon)**	1. a cart used for carrying heavy loads 2. a railway truck	
waist	the middle of the body	
waistcoat	a sleeveless garment worn under a jacket	
wait for	to stay in a place until something happens	**waited** **waiting**
wait on	to serve food at a table	**waiter** **waiting** **waitress**
wake	to stop sleeping	**waking** **woke** **woken**
walk	to go on foot	**walked** **walker** **walking**
wall	1. a fence made of brick, stone or concrete 2. the side of a room or building	**walled**
wallaby	a small kangaroo	**wallabies**
wallet	a thin pocket case, usually made of leather	
walrus	a large sea animal like a seal	**walruses**
wand	a long, thin rod	
wander	to move slowly along in no special direction	**wandered** **wandering**
want	1. to need 2. to wish for	**wanted** **wanting**
war	when armies fight	

wardrobe	a tall cupboard for storing clothes	
warehouse	a building for storing things	
warm	neither hot nor cold	**warmer** **warmest** **warmly** **warmth**
warn	to tell someone about the danger of anything	**warned** **warning**
warrior	a person who has done a lot of fighting in war	
wash	to take dirt off anything by cleaning with water	**washed** **washer** **washes** **washing**
wasp	a black and yellow flying insect that stings	
waste	1. something that is useless 2. not to use up 3. to use up carelessly	**wasted** **wasteful** **wasting**
watch	1. a small clock that you wear, usually on the wrist 2. to keep your eyes fixed on something	**watches** **watched** **watches** **watching**
watchman	a person who guards a building	**watchmen**
water	a liquid which we drink	**waterless** **watery**
waterfall	a place where water tumbles from one level to another	
waterproof	not allowing water to pass through	
wave	1. a moving line of water on the sea or on a lake 2. a curve or curl in your hair 3. to flutter something	**waved** **waving** **wavy**
wax	used for making candles	
way	1. a path or road 2. how to do something	**wayside**

weak	not strong	**weaker** **weakest** **weakling** **weakly** **weakness**
wealth	all that a rich person has	**wealthier** **wealthiest** **wealthy**
weapon	a tool to fight with	
wear	1. to be dressed in something 2. to rub away	**wearing** **worn**
weary	tired	**wearily** **weariness**
weasel	a long thin wild animal	
weather	(The *weather* was sunny)	
weathercock	the shape of a cock on a pointer, which turns to show from which way the wind is blowing	
weave	to make cloth by passing threads under and over one another	**weaving** **woven**
wedding	when people get married	
Wednesday	the fourth day of the week	
weed	1. a wild plant growing where it is not wanted 2. to take out unwanted plants	**weeded** **weeding** **weed-killer**
week	seven days	**weekday** **weekend** **weekly**
weep	to cry	**weeping** **wept**
weigh	to find out how heavy anything is	**weighed** **weighing** **weight**
welcome	to show you are pleased when someone comes	**welcomed** **welcoming**

well	1. a deep hole in the ground from which water or oil can be got 2. in good health 3. in a proper manner
wept	(The boy *wept* because his dog was lost)
were	(John and Mary *were* six yesterday)
west	where the sun sets: the opposite to the east **western**
whale	a very large sea animal
wharf	a place where ships load and unload **wharves**
what	(Sally did not know *what* to do) **whatever**
wheat	a plant whose seeds are used to make flour
wheel	1. a circle of wood or metal which turns on a rod **wheeled** **wheeling** 2. to push anything on wheels
wheelbarrow	a hand-cart with one wheel
when	1. (I shall come in *when* it rains) **whenever** 2. (*When* will you be there?)
where	(This is *where* I put the book) **whereabouts** **wherever**
whether	(*Whether* we win or lose the final, we will get a medal)
which	1. (*Which* of these is yours?) **whichever** 2. (That is the desk *which* you will have)
while	1. (We shall be good *while* the teacher is out) 2. (In a little *while* it will be time to go)
whip	1. a piece of thin cord or leather on a stick used for striking **whipped** **whipping** 2. to strike with a whip

whirlwind	a very strong wind that blows round and round, and may cause great damage	
whiskers	1. hairs growing on a man's cheek 2. the long, bristly hairs which grow above the mouth on some animals	
whisper	to talk in a very quiet voice	**whispered** **whispering**
whistle	1. a wind instrument like a small pipe 2. to make a sharp high sound with the mouth	**whistled** **whistling**
white	the colour of snow	**whiter** **whitest**
whitewash	a sort of watery white paint for covering walls and ceilings	**white-washed**
who	1. (*Who* spilt the ink?) 2. (It was Jim *who* was there)	**whom** **whose**
whole	1. every part of a thing 2. undamaged: complete	
why	for what reason?	
wick	the cotton part of a candle or oil-lamp, which is lit	
wicked	evil: bad	
wicket	three stumps in a game of cricket	
wide	broad	**wider** **widest**
widow	a woman whose husband is dead	
widower	a man whose wife is dead	
width	how wide a thing is	
wife	a married woman	**wives**
wigwam	a tent used by Red Indians	
wild	untamed: fierce	**wildly**
wilful	1. wanting one's own way 2. done on purpose	**wilfully**

will	1. the power to choose what to do 2. (*Will* you go?)	
willing	ready to do what you are asked	**willingly**
willow	a tree which grows near water	
wilt	to droop	**wilted** **wilting**
win	to gain a victory	**winner** **winning** **won**
wind	1. air that moves quickly 2. to wrap round tightly 3. to twist in and out	**windier** **windiest** **winding** **windmill** **windscreen** **windy** **wound**
window	a space in the wall to let in air and light	**window-sill**
wine	a drink usually made from grapes or fruit	
wing	the part of a bird that is spread out when the bird flies	**winged**
wink	to move one eyelid up and down	**winked** **winking**
winter	the season between autumn and spring	**wintry**
wipe	to dry or clean something with a cloth	**wiped** **wiper** **wiping**
wire	a thin metal thread	**wired** **wireless** **wiring**
wise	sensible	**wisdom** **wisely**
wish	1. (Cinderella's *wish* was granted when she went to the Ball) 2. to want something	**wishes** **wished** **wishes** **wishful** **wishing**

witch	a woman who is supposed to do magic	**witches**
with	(Mary came to school *with* Susan)	**within** **without**
witness	someone who was watching when something happened	**witnesses**
witty	funny in a clever way	
wizard	a man who is supposed to do magic	
wobble	to rock from side to side	**wobbled** **wobbling**
woke	(The sun was shining when I *woke* up in the morning)	
wolf	a wild animal like a large dog	**wolves**
woman	a female	**women**
won	(Our team *won* the Cup)	
wonder	1. amazement 2. something causing amazement 3. to be curious	**wondered** **wonderful** **wondering**
wood	1. the trunk and branches of a tree 2. a large group of trees	**wooded** **wooden** **woodland** **woodwork**
woodpecker	a bird that taps a tree with its beak to find insects for food	
wool	1. the hairy coat of a sheep 2. the thread made from wool	**woollen** **woolly**
word	a sound or group of letters that has a definite meaning	
wore	(She *wore* a blue coat)	
work	1. a job 2. to do a job of some kind	**worked** **worker** **working** **workshop**
worker	a person who works, usually with tools	
world	the earth and everything on it	
worm	a small animal with no legs, that wriggles along	

worn	1. showing signs of wear 2. (I have not *worn* this hat yet)	
worry	1. care 2. to be troubled about something 3. to annoy	**worries** **worried** **worries** **worrying**
worse	less good	
worst	the least good	
worth	1. of the same value as 2. deserving of	**worthless** **worthy**
would	(He *would* like to help me)	
wound	1. damage to the skin 2. to damage someone's skin 3. (John *wound* a ball of wool)	**wounded** **wounding**
woven	made of threads crossed over and under each other	
wrap	to cover round	**wrapped** **wrapper** **wrapping**
wreck	1. something that has been damaged or completely ruined 2. to make a wreck of something	**wreckage** **wrecked** **wrecking**
wren	a very small bird	
wrestle	1. to try to force someone to the ground by struggling with him 2. to struggle with	**wrestled** **wrestler** **wrestling**
wriggle	to move by twisting and turning	**wriggled** **wriggler** **wriggling**
wring	to squeeze by twisting	**wringer** **wringing** **wrung**
wrinkle	1. a crease 2. to make a wrinkle	**wrinkled** **wrinkling**
wrist	the joint between the hand and the arm	

write	to form words or figures so that they can be read	**writing** **written** **wrote**
wrong	not right	**wrongly**
wrote	(I *wrote* a letter to my aunt)	
wrung	(Jim *wrung* the clothes to squeeze out the water)	

x

x-rays	rays used to take photographs which show what your body is like underneath your skin
xylophone	a musical instrument made of bars of wood which are hit with hammers

y

yacht	a light boat with large sails	**yachting**
yard	1. measure of length 2. enclosed ground, usually near a building	
yawn	to take a deep breath through the mouth because you feel tired	**yawned** **yawning**
year	twelve months: fifty-two weeks: three hundred and sixty-five days: the time that the earth takes to go round the sun	**yearly**
yell	to shout or scream very loudly	**yelled** **yelling**
yellow	the colour of buttercup flowers	
yesterday	the day before today	

yet	1. so far
	2. however
yew	an evergreen tree
yolk	the yellow part of an egg
you	('Who are *you*?' I said to him)
young	not grown up

younger
youngest

your	belonging to you
youth	1. the time after childhood
	2. a young person

youthful

Z

zebra	an African animal like a horse, but with a striped coat
zero	nought
zigzag	to turn sharply from side to side as you go along

zigzagged
zigzagging

zip-fastener	a fastener with a sliding catch
zoo	a place where wild animals are kept in pens or cages

METRIC MEASURES

millimetre (mm)   gram (g)

centimetre (cm)   kilogram (kg)

metre (m)   tonne (t)

kilometre (km)   litre (l)

MATHEMATICAL SIGNS

plus $+$ is approximately equal to $\simeq$

minus $-$ degree $^\circ$

multiplied by $\times$ percentage $\%$

divided by $\div$ therefore $\therefore$

is equal to $=$ square root $\sqrt{}$

is not equal to $\neq$

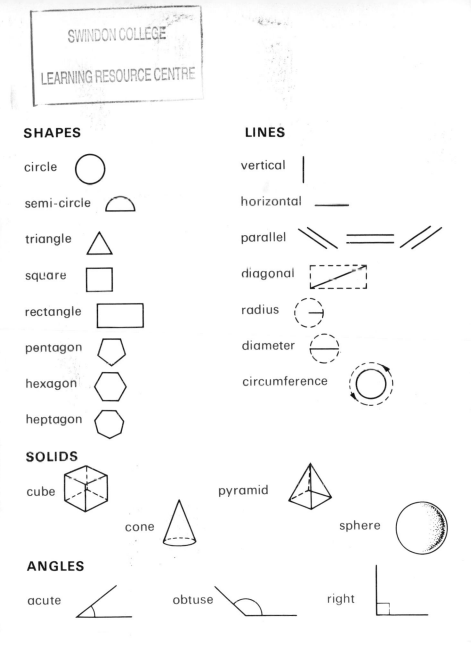

SHAPES

circle

semi-circle

triangle

square

rectangle

pentagon

hexagon

heptagon

LINES

vertical

horizontal

parallel

diagonal

radius

diameter

circumference

SOLIDS

cube

cone

pyramid

sphere

ANGLES

acute

obtuse

right